Transformational Mentoring

CREATING DEVELOPMENTAL ALLIANCES FOR CHANGING ORGANIZATIONAL CULTURES

Julie Hay

To Lesley,

with best wishes and thanks

for your interest.

Julie Hay

October 1995

McGRAW-HILL BOOK COMPANY

London · New York · St Louis · San Francisco · Auckland
Bogotá · Caracas · Lisbon · Madrid · Mexico · Milan
Montreal · New Delhi · Panama · Paris · San Juan · São Paulo
Singapore · Sydney · Tokyo · Toronto

Published by McGraw-Hill Book Company Europe
Shoppenhangers Road, Maidenhead, Berkshire, SL6 2QL, England
Telephone 01628 23432
Fax 01628 770224

British Library Cataloguing in Publication Data
Hay, Julie
 Transformational Mentoring: Creating
 Developmental Alliances for Changing Organizational Cultures
 I. Title
 158.7

 ISBN 0–07–707627–3

Library of Congress Cataloging-in-Publication Data
Hay, Julie.
 Transformational mentoring: creating developmental alliances for changing organiza-
tional cultures / Julie Hay.
  p. cm.
 Includes index.
 ISBN 0–07–707627–3
 1. Mentoring in business. 2. Career development. 3. Organizational change. I. Title.
 HF5385.H3 1995
 658.4'07124–dc20   95–22721
                                                                                    CIP

12345 BL 998765

Typeset by Computape (Pickering) Ltd, North Yorkshire
and printed and bound in Great Britain by Biddles Limited, Guildford

Printed on permanent paper in compliance with ISO Standard 9706.

Contents

Preface

Hay Health Warning No. 1
Reading this book may seriously damage your paradigm!
This book is about a new approach to human development. It is an approach that requires us to adopt different models of human and organizational functioning. I know that many people have done so already—and I will quote from several of them as we go on. However, I also recognize that much of the literature around *transformation* can seem very esoteric, especially if you work in a traditional, hierarchical, macho organization. Transformation smacks of 'touchy-feely'—with terms like new age, spirituality, love and so on being quite enough to scare off many practical, down-to-earth managers and professionals. It has the same effect on me sometimes, even as I write about it!

However, I think we are caught up in an inevitable, and welcome, move towards people being able to access their true potential. This may seem unlikely when we consider the recent recession which appears to have blanketed most of the Western world. Even so, there are trends now which indicate that people are expecting a more *human* quality of life. Perhaps the recession has even been a contributor—if life gets too bad people are likely to rebel and seek to change things in ways that they might not if things are still bearable.

Hence this book, which I hope will challenge and stimulate you to change the way you view the process of individual development, the nature of organizations, the function of mentoring, and perhaps even the meaning of life!

Hay Health Warning No. 2
This book contains new, untested ideas
Charles Handy has been quoted as saying that he does not give details of specific organizations in his books because it is unfair to them. Tom Peters still quotes specific organizations, even though those that he refers to as excellent have a habit of becoming considerably less so soon afterwards (I heard that at least one company refused to be named in case there really is a jinx).

I do not quote examples of organizations applying the ideas in this book because there are none as yet—the ideas are still too new. There are several who have started to explore the developmental alliance approach and will probably know a lot more about it by the time this book is published; however, as I write they are in the early stages only. Appendix 1 gives details of a mentoring network, which will no doubt continue to be one of the ways in which the Human Resources (HR) professionals involved share their experiences.

So, if you are an innovator, let me know how you get on! If you prefer caution, take note that most of the frameworks and skills have all been used successfully in other contexts, so the only difficult part will be transferring them across to a developmental alliance mode—and I have included various suggestions and checklists to guide you. If, in spite of that, you are still hesitant about going it alone, you can always contact me or a member of the network for help with implementation.

Hay Health Warning No. 3
This book is full of jargon and donkey bridges!
I have anticipated that my readers will be professionals and managers who are already interested in individual and organizational development. This is not intended as a book for beginners! I have therefore assumed a certain amount of prior exposure to current thinking in these areas. However, as I also realize that every reader may not be familiar with every concept, I have indicated sources of further information.

Because my background is as a trainer, I do my best to present information in ways which aid recall. I therefore use donkey bridges, or *Eselsbrücken*, as they are called in German—those gimmicky plays on words or letters that serve as brain markers when we want to remember something. For an interesting description of the benefits of donkey bridges, see John Townsend's article 'Making Messages Memorable' in *Training and Development Journal*, January 1994.

If you hate alliteration, and John's article doesn't convince you how useful donkey bridges are, please feel free to change the words each time you come to lists starting with the same letter. Please remember also that misery is optional—you choose how much energy to invest in feeling annoyed each time.

Why transformational mentoring?

Organizational transformation and mentoring

I hesitated over calling this book *Transformational Mentoring*. I was aware that organizational development (OD) had been superseded by organizational transformation (OT) (see Appendix 2 if OT is new to you); that OD had become OT. However, transformational mentoring seemed such a big concept. I worried that people might be put off by it, or would not know what it meant, or that it might raise expectations that would not be met when they read the book!

However, the more I learned about organizational transformation, the more I recognized that the vocabulary employed to write about OT contained similar words and phrases to those I had been using to talk about a new approach to mentoring that I believed was needed. Community, shared values and visions, creating learning organizations, changing the paradigm—all seemed relevant. Then, just as I was due to produce the final draft, I attended a conference in India and found myself listening to a speaker talking about transformation—clearly an omen (or at least a sign that this shift in paradigm is happening in many places).

Shortly afterwards, another omen—I was asked by a psychotherapist colleague if I would be interested in co-training with him at Esalen, an early home of the human potential movement in California, because programmes were being run there for business groups. This type of audience for Esalen had been predicted by Frank Rose in *Fortune* magazine back in October 1990, when he pointed out that US corporations were entering a new age. Frank called this 'the New Age without the glazed look', making it clear that it was not about some of the more esoteric New Age ideas but that it was a new paradigm which incorporated love and idealism in the workplace.

Although the OT philosophies match the way that I believe mentoring should function, my ideas for a new approach arose first from a much more pragmatic set of considerations. It seemed to me that we were going to run out of mentors anyway! In the traditional mentoring model, we need older, wiser, senior managers to groom young high-flying protégés. Yet organizations are getting flatter and leaner all the time and change is happening at such a rate that:

- there will not be enough senior managers to go round
- those that there are will not have had the right experience (and there is probably no such thing any more as the 'right' experience)
- change is coming so fast that we can't be certain what will be needed
- career channels are fast disappearing
- the old role models are being seen as outmoded
- the old boy network is discriminatory
- employees who are not high flyers still expect opportunities for development
- an increasing number of people are self-employed yet still want mentoring
- cloning existing managers will not help create new organizational cultures
- cloning existing white, male managers leads to indirect discrimination
- no sensible person wants to mould themself to fit an organization which might make them redundant tomorrow
- people are more aware of the advantages of networking.

These general trends were highlighted for me by some very specific examples:

- A computer manufacturing company which needed ways to maintain the morale and motivation of technical staff whose promotion prospects had virtually disappeared after cuts in the numbers of managerial jobs.
- A local authority running action learning projects where it became clear that team members took far more notice of the peer feedback they received during the programme than they had ever taken of the performance appraisals carried out by their managers.
- Management mentors in a major bank who began to question their role when they realized that branch managers of the future would follow a very different career path—so how could they sensibly give advice based on their own experiences?
- A number of professional associations which have developed mentoring networks so that members can link up with each other— including the chance to have a mentor who works in a different organization.

Developmental alliances

It seems, therefore, that we need to rethink the way that mentoring operates. I propose that we introduce a new approach which will make the benefits of mentoring available to anyone who wants them.

I have named this approach a *developmental alliance*, which I define as:

> a relationship between equals in which one or more of those involved is enabled to:
>
> increase awareness,
> identify alternatives and
> initiate action
>
> to develop themselves.

The key word here is *equals*. Instead of the traditional mentoring arrangement of older, wiser mentor with young protégé, I am suggesting that we rewrite the title of David Clutterbuck's book *Everyone Needs a Mentor*[1] and say instead that *Everyone Can* Have *a Mentor*. This will allow us to draw our mentors from a much wider pool than just managers. We could even look outside the organization, and outside the organizational context, to have mentors who bring different experiences of life to the task. The *skills* of mentoring will be much more important in the corporate world of the future than (potentially outdated) experience—and I am convinced that most people can learn the necessary skills.

It would also be far more in keeping with current thinking about human capacities. An underlying philosophy of organizational transformation, learning companies and so on is that we all have an inner drive to grow and develop. Organizations are not always structured to take this into account. Eric Berne[2], the originator of transactional analysis, suggested that there is an energy source within us, which he called *physis*. This is the human equivalent of the way in which plants continue to grow towards the sun. We know that plants do this even when obstacles are put in their way—they grow around them. Humans can do this, too, if we have an approach that lets us grow in a direction we choose ourselves, and not one imposed by someone else because it suits the needs of the organization.

Many people grow up in an environment which discourages physis. They are taught instead to conform and to stay within boundaries, to stay in their place. This is like pouring concrete over the ground—any seeds trapped below will not germinate. Fortunately, if the concrete is cracked the plants will start to grow as soon as they are exposed. People are the same—take a pickaxe to the concrete of organizational constraints, chip away at the artificial barriers imposed during the educational process, and people will seize the opportunity to grow.

Tom Peters[3] gives us several examples of this when he reports on companies such as Titeflex, which delayered and at one point reduced supervisor numbers and created self-managed cells over a weekend! Union Pacific Railroad took longer, at 90 days, but stripped out five layers in a department of 30 000. In spite of the 'accepted wisdom' about the way in which people oppose change, these and other organizations have discovered that their employees *welcome* major restructurings that give them the chance to take on more responsibility.

Perhaps this is why neuro-linguistic programming (NLP), Gestalt and transactional analysis are becoming increasingly popular as training models within organizations. Neuro-linguistic programming captures the essence within its *presuppositions*[4] of:

- People have all the resources they need.
- People make the best choices available to them.

The Gestalt approach has a similar message; the 'I-You' approach is based on several assumptions[5], including:

- We are complete packages; we have a body, thoughts, perceptions, sensations and emotions that are interrelated.
- We are proactive and therefore determine our own responses to the world (even though we may seem to be reactive).
- We are capable of being aware of our own perceptions, sensations, thoughts and emotions.
- We have the resources and potential to satisfy our needs.

Transactional analysis[6] has a basic principle of 'I'm OK, You're OK', a goal of autonomy rather than an unconsciously scripted life, the concept of physis and the notion of an aspiration arrow which emerges through our ego states and represents our growth.

I mentioned that this is a somewhat controversial approach. I remember in particular a very lively discussion at a certain meeting of a certain branch of Companions and Fellows of the Institute of Personnel Management, at which considerable doubts were expressed about the ability of ordinary people to help each other in this way. Equally interesting was a workshop for group process trainers at which the view was expressed that people were not capable of changing themselves! I did wonder whether both sets of opinions were perhaps influenced just a little by a concern that trainers and personnel managers would become superfluous. ...

There was a decidedly different response from many other personnel and training professionals with whom I talked. I found that there was considerable interest in developing the approach. Most of the human resource managers I met said that they had been exploring, working on or struggling with similar ideas. There was a lot of curiosity about what others were doing, so that I was able to set up a network for sharing. This now meets quarterly, and current membership includes many large, well-known organizations in the public and private sectors (more members are welcome: see Appendix 1 for details).

Notes

1. Clutterbuck, David, *Everyone Needs a Mentor*, Institute of Personnel Management, 2nd edn, 1991.
2. Berne, Eric, *A Layman's Guide to Psychiatry and Psychoanalysis*, Penguin, 1971. For a very helpful treatment of this concept, see also Clarkson, Petruska, *Transactional Analysis Psychotherapy*, Routledge, 1992.
3. Peters, Tom, *Liberation Management*, Macmillan, 1992.
4. Ideas on presuppositions based on the *Practitioners Training Manual 1992* by Pace Personal Development Ltd, London (reproduced with permission from Bretto, Charlotte C., *A Framework for Excellence*, 1988). For more information about NLP, see also O'Connor, J. and Seymour, J., *Introducing Neuro-Linguistic Programming*, Mandala, 1990.
5. See Clarkson, Petruska, *Gestalt Counselling in Action*, Sage, 1989. For a succinct description of the Gestalt view, see also McKewn, Jennifer, 'Modern Gestalt—an Integrative and Ethical Approach to Counselling and Psychotherapy' in the *Journal of the British Association for Counselling*, Vol. 5, No. 2, May 1994.
6. For a helpful overview of the range of TA concepts, see Stewart, I. and Joines, V., *TA Today*, Lifespace Publishing, 1988.

Checklist: Your own situation

Before you read on, take a few minutes to consider your responses to the following prompts.

■ What trends are affecting your organization—now and in the foreseeable future?
■ What is being done to develop individuals within the organization to handle these trends?
■ How do recruitment and promotion processes take the trends into account?
■ What reinforcement and recognition is given to individuals who show a commitment to developing themselves?
■ Is there a mentoring scheme? If so, who are the mentors and who are the mentees?
■ Are there informal mentors? If so, again who are the mentors and the mentees?
■ Are development and/or mentoring opportunities widely available or

are they restricted to a selected few? What impact does this have on the organization?

■ Do you have a mentor? Are you a mentor to someone else? Have you been a mentor or a mentee in the past?

■ What benefits and drawbacks do you associate with mentoring?

Trends: The organizational perspective

Development or transformation?

As we move from organizational development to organizational transformation, we have to make a paradigm shift. I understand paradigm shift to mean that we change to such a different model for perceiving the world that we realize we have shifted to a different level of awareness. I read somewhere that transformation is to development as marketing is to sales; I think this fails to capture the significance of the shift. Perhaps it is more like the difference between knowing the sea as a fish within it, compared to knowing it as Columbus did. Or like the change of view, and corresponding increase in spirituality, described by astronauts after they have looked back at Earth from space.

I like the definition given by Schaef and Fassel[1] in their excellent book on addictive organizations (page 38):

> *a paradigm shift is a move away from the certainty of the right answers to a*
> *process of transformation and a world of the unknown.*

This matches a more personal example of a paradigm shift—when I first realized many years ago that the highly successful assessment centres which I had researched, designed and run for an engineering organization were, in fact, simply reinforcing the view of managerial effectiveness that already existed in that same company and that would not serve them so well in the future! We had managers who were effective, we conducted our research carefully to identify their characteristics and competence, and we then set about finding new managers who matched the profile. Only later did I recognize the way that this reinforced the existing culture.

So one of the trends affecting organizations is this need for a paradigm shift. We need to *transform* organizations and individuals instead of developing them. We need to change the things we do rather than change the way we do things.

Which metaphor?

One way of understanding the nature of the paradigm shift we need is to consider the metaphors we use. Gareth Morgan[2,3] provides us with a selection of images for organizations: as machines, as organisms, as brains, as cultures, as political systems, as psychic prisons, as flux and transformation, as instruments of domination and as spider plants.

Depending on the metaphors we use (often unconsciously), we understand organizations very differently. If we use spider plants, Morgan suggests that we can think of head office in the large pot, with umbilical cords connecting it to the satellites. Using a machine metaphor, however, might lead to assumptions about workers being no more than cogs, while the political systems image captures the essence of organizational lobbying and politicking.

This range of options means that we may well be using a different metaphor to our colleagues. An appropriate comparison might be with the way in which an army of ants might make sense of an elephant. The recognition of this difference in images is itself part of a paradigm shift—previously there tended to be a few metaphors only, which were shared by many people. Now many are on the quest for new and different ways to construe an organization.

The metaphor of flux and transformation is currently popular. It also has a long history—the Greek philosopher, Heraclitus, way back around 500 BC, was probably first with his metaphor of a river in which the waters are continually flowing. This gives both permanence and change—the river remains, but the water in it is never the same.

Bohm[4] took this further when he extended the metaphor to the universe and introduced terms like *holomovement* and *holoflux* to cover the appearance of stability that is created by change. *Fractals* have also been added—an easily accessible example to show how these identical patterns are created at ever decreasing (or increasing) levels is the cauliflower. Cut it open, and then into smaller pieces, and you can see the repeating pattern.

A recent survey by Ashridge Management Research Group[5] asked leading executives to share their visions and strategies. The results show clearly that these executives will need to operate with a metaphor of change—the following are some of the themes that emerged:

■ bewildered by so many developments
■ now all happening at once instead of one at a time
■ coping with unpredictability, change, discontinuity
■ can no longer plan long-term due to the pace of change
■ so many issues are interrelated, need to integrate, understand relationships of parts to the whole.

This is almost the opposite to the kind of situation envisaged within traditional mentoring arrangements. There the expectation is that the mentor has valuable personal experience of the organizational environment and can pass this on to the mentee. Unfortunately, as Heraclitus said, you cannot step into the same river twice because the water keeps flowing past. Being in an organization even as recently as two years ago is long enough in many cases now for our experience to have become outdated. And the faster the river flows, the quicker we lose touch.

With a paradigm shift and a different metaphor, we can also see that it may not be a river any more. The list of issues produced in the Ashridge survey sounds rather as if the executives have been shifted into the ocean, or placed beneath a waterfall. Even skills in dealing with corporate sharks are not much use unless you can at least keep your head above water long enough to breathe!

Megatrends for women

One way in which the river is changing is through the trend towards greater involvement of women in public life. Patricia Aburdene and John Naisbitt[6] have devoted a whole book to describing the ways in which women 'are overturning centuries of male domination' and showing how 'women's inspirational leadership in business will replace outdated management hierarchies'. They believe that the women's movement has reached a critical mass—a point at which there can be no turning back.

There are several items in their book which have direct relevance to the future of mentoring:

- more women in public life
- more women entrepreneurs
- more networking
- changing expectations of girls.

The first of these concerns the greater involvement of women in politics, religion, sport, business and social activism. Women bring different values and priorities to these areas—and in doing so they are changing the very environment in which organizations have to function. Women expect to create structures and institutions where collaboration and partnership are the norm. As they become increasingly influential in public life they will have a major impact on the legal aspects of running a business, on the contribution which religion makes to shaping people's expectations, and on the general frame of reference which people adopt when judging the quality of organizational behaviour. In other words, the critical mass of women will change the paradigm.

The second item echoes this shift in paradigm. Aburdene and Naisbitt point out the irrelevance of using standards such as the Fortune 500 to measure business success. They tell us that the companies of the '500 list' are not the greater, or the most dynamic, part of the US economy. Instead, far more of the US Gross Domestic Product (GDP) is contributed by small to medium-sized firms. Even more noteworthy is the fact that more than 5 million American women lead small to medium-sized companies, creating many new jobs each year while the larger corporations are cutting back.

These new businesses are likely to remain smaller, or at least to retain smaller units, because they will be created to a female model—a model which incorporates closeness and genuine connection. An interesting example of this is given by Aburdene and Naisbitt when they point out that the female leaders of the Norwegian political parties called each other by their first names during a televised debate, whereas their male counterparts would have been more formal (and less collaborative).

There is every reason to assume that these US trends are occurring elsewhere even though we may not have the data to confirm it. We have already seen the increase in women in the political sphere around the world: Corazon Aquino, Khaleda Zia, Benazir Bhutto, Violetta Chamorro, Mary Robinson, Gro Bruntland, Indira Gandhi, Golda Meir, Margaret Thatcher, these are some of the best known examples. It is even rumoured that a child in the UK, having only ever known Margaret Thatcher's consecutive terms in office, asked whether a man could be a Prime Minister!

These two trends—the changing political and social environment and the increasing female entrepreneurship—will combine to change the nature of mentoring. Mentors used to the 'old order' will become obsolete; no-one will need to learn from them how to operate in a climate that no longer applies. The style of mentoring will also have to change, as there will be little benefit from acquiring typically male approaches to functioning in a competitive hierarchy. The way that mentoring is provided will also shift, with a greater tendency to look for mentors *outside* smaller organizations.

This will link with the third trend—more networking. Networking, peer coaching and co-counselling are just some of the topics that are becoming increasingly popular in the pop psychology/personal development literature. Again, this is a trend much influenced by women's values. It has a very different feel to it from the 'old boy' networks of the past.

Although we could argue that both involve doing favours, the current approaches focus more on opportunities and help with learning and growth, whereas the 'old boy' network was about finding jobs for the boys (and their relatives), setting up mutually beneficial business deals, or planning the 'arranged marriages' of the corporate world. Some of this has even become illegal as anti-trust and monopolies legislation moves us towards more ethical ways of doing business.

Finally, the fourth trend worth particular mention is the way that girls' expectations are changing. There has now been ample research to show that girls are being programmed to have low self-esteem regarding certain subjects that are seen as male preserves. This has at last meant that teachers and parents can actively redress the balance. We can therefore expect that more young women in future will start their working lives with expectations of having challenging and satisfying jobs and careers.

They will need mentors! But these will not be older, white, male mentors. Nor will they want as their mentors those women who have succeeded in the corporate world by adopting the male characteristics which created the competitive hierarchies in the first place. They will want role models who can demonstrate the effectiveness of 'women's' values, who can function as mentors in a style which encourages self-development, collaboration and genuine connectiveness, and who operate as equals when mentoring, regardless of the respective levels of prior experience or achievement.

The decency decade

Another writer who alerts us to current trends that will have a major impact on life in organizations is Faith Popcorn[7]. In the intriguingly titled *Popcorn Report*, she refers to the nineties in the USA as the *decency decade*, in which we have to sell the company as much as we sell its products.

Among 10 trends she identifies is the concept of the *vigilante consumer*. These are the protesters, becoming more and more influential, who will demand organizations with human faces. Companies will need to show that they are actively caring for the environment, that they operate according to codes of ethics, and that they admit to mistakes and take prompt action to put matters right. Popcorn gives as an example the impact of consumer boycotts on tuna until the industry stopped using the drift nets which killed dolphins. She also tells us that Esso lost 10 000 credit card customers because of its handling of the Alaska oil spill.

The way in which organizations, and mentors, interpret the decency/vigilante metaphor will be crucial. Those who link it to concepts such as environmental stewardship may well work to a holistic model, in which all stakeholders share a common aim in protecting the world and its resources. These resources will include people, so that the organization will treat employees with respect. These will also be the organizations which reflect such beliefs in mission statements that are based on shared values.

However, it is just as easy to choose a decency/vigilante metaphor that is a reflection of the Wild West. In that case, managers and mentors will operate a culture in which the good guys don't shoot people in the back and where vigilantes take the law into their own hands and sometimes lynch innocent people. Traditional mentoring under such a metaphor would consist of passing on the skills of being quick on the draw, shooting the bad guys (in the front), and doing this before the vigilantes can act. Rather like the required resignations of executives when organizational mistakes are discovered.

The learning organization

Another major factor signalling the need for a new form of mentoring is the advent of learning organizations. Perhaps I should refer instead to the *current* vogue for learning organizations—in their book *The Learning Company*[8] Mike Pedler, John Burgoyne and Tom Boydell provide us with a history lesson that takes the idea back to Moses (via Bateson, Gardner, Lippitt, Schon, Argyris, Revans and even Peters and Waterman who didn't seem to realize the significance at the time).

Pedler and colleagues define a learning company as 'an organization that facilitates the learning of all its members and continuously transforms itself'. In spite of the historical references, they point out that the learning company is still at the idea stage and there is not as yet an established body of case study examples to demonstrate various approaches. They provide us with 11 dimensions, which they cluster into strategy, looking in, structure, looking out and learning opportunities.

- For *strategy,* they provide a deliberate learning approach for policy and strategy formulation with experiments, feedback loops and modifications as the normal process. They suggest that *all* members of the company take part in policy formulation.
- For *looking in,* they recommend that information technology and financial control systems are both used as sources of information and aids to learning. They also suggest more communication across instead of down the organization, plus reward systems that reward flexibility.
- When it comes to *structure,* they again suggest flexibility—this time in terms of roles, careers and departmental boundaries that allow experimentation and adaptation.
- *Looking out* comprises using boundary workers as environmental scanners and participating with suppliers, customers and competitors in inter-company learning.
- Finally, *learning opportunities* are identified specifically (having been evident in other clusters) as having a learning climate in which people are expected to be always learning and improving, supported by the provisions of self-development opportunities for everyone.

How then might the learning company affect the role of mentors? For a start, there are implicit assumptions that we are *all* capable of learning—and that we need to share that learning with others in the organization. Mentoring schemes (and, indeed, training and development programmes) which are restricted to the chosen few are not enough. Also, mentors will need to recognize more clearly than some do now that the mentoring process involves learning for mentee *and* mentor.

There will be an additional impact on the mentoring role arising from the involvement in policy formulation and the environmental scanning. Both of these will result in employees being more influential when it comes to the making of corporate decisions. To do this involves a much greater involvement in and knowledge of the goals of the company. They might *just* be able to acquire some of this knowledge from a traditional mentor to start with—but fairly soon they will know as much about it themselves and will no longer need a guide to the 'corporate politics'.

Furthermore, if they are capable of sharing information and learning, and of understanding company strategies, then they are capable of helping others. We will therefore have a much greater pool of potential mentors, each of whom will have the ability to assist their colleagues to maximise their own learning. Pedler *et al*'s preference for learning *company* rather than learning organization reflects this—they choose the word 'company' to emphasize that it is about being *together*, in the company of others.

This notion will also be essential for the second element in the learning organization definition—that it 'continuously transforms itself'. To do this requires more than simply enabling individuals to learn for themselves. It will need a change of paradigm, so that employees (and other stakeholders) recognize that they *are* the organization in so far as the organization consists of the interactions just as much as the fixed resources.

Organizations which truly become learning companies will therefore consist of people who challenge and change things, who are continually looking for new perspectives, and who make constant shifts in their thinking and behaviour.

Adaptors or innovators?

Michael Kirton[9] provides an elegant way of understanding this, with his questionnaire that measures tendencies to adapt or innovate. *Adaptors* are great for keeping the show on the road, while *innovators* challenge the status quo. Both are creative but in different ways—adaptors introduce new and better ways of doing things; innovators introduce new and better things to do.

Kirton emphasizes the strength of each style and points out that organizations need both, particularly because they counterbalance each other's weaknesses. Thus, left on their own adaptors would continue to improve efficiency at providing goods or services which customers have ceased to desire. Innovators, on the other hand, would bring in exciting new products or services, but then fail to take care of getting them to the market.

I suspect that traditional mentoring schemes have been best suited to adaptors, for both mentors and mentees. Innovator mentors, on the other hand, are likely to have shown little regard for the customary practices in their organizations, and therefore have been seen as less than helpful to their mentees. Innovator mentees may well have had somewhat un-orthodox tendencies and been seen by their mentors as undisciplined or even rebellious.

Kirton reckons that the adaptor/innovator continuum spans a normal distribution curve, so there will have been many mentors and mentees who were 'average'. He states also that we can relate to others up to half a standard deviation away. This may well have helped with communication—but it will also have led to a certain degree of mediocrity within the mentoring process.

An example in a local authority concerned an action learning programme. The chief executive was an innovator, and the organization was attempting to move into a more 'innovator' style of working. There was a corporate vision emphasizing individual initiative and responsibility. Within this setting, action learning sets were given investigative projects to do. Two major difficulties arose, although both were so much a part of the culture that they were easy to miss.

First, certain of the chief officers, who were the project clients, were adaptors. They were committed to the action learning process but, as adaptors, were doing it because 'good' chief officers support their chief executive (even if he or she does have unusual notions!). However, without realizing it they tended to reject any overt signs of innovator behaviour within the sets. Their expectations, and their evaluations of the project presentations, were biased towards more effective ways of doing the same things as in the past.

Suggestions for radical change were discouraged. In one case the constraints regarding the conduct of a project totally emasculated the team. They expected to consider new uses for a council-owned site—but were then told that an extension of the existing lease was already being renegotiated and that they should confine themselves to recommendations on better ways to continue providing the same facilities.

The second problem was related to the typical local authority decision-making process. The sets were only allowed to investigate and recommend—they could not implement because any significant changes had to be put to the appropriate committee. By the time the approval was obtained the sets had been disbanded. In addition, the tight controls associated with the spending of public money meant that even innovator chief officers could not delegate their responsibilities.

The action learning programme was in itself a form of mentoring, albeit with a group rather than individuals. It remained as a very traditional mentoring process because of the high level of adaptor preferences. Set members were encouraged to learn but within the accepted norms. They spent time with their chief officer clients, agreeing terms of reference, discussing their ideas, presenting their suggestions. The client acted as a role model for how one successfully 'manages' the internal (and external) politics of such an organization—with a strong emphasis on how it had been done for so many years.

It was not until some new chief officers were recruited externally that innovators were added to the top team. The nature of the projects, and the mentoring provided, then changed style.

The stages of an organization

To be true learning companies, organizations need to have reached a stage where people can make genuine contact with each other. Scott Peck, in *The Different Drum*[10], writes of our need for community. Although he points out that community cannot be defined in one sentence, he refers to:

■ communicating honestly with each other
■ having deeper relationships
■ sharing commitments to rejoice and mourn together.

I extend a model developed by Valerie Stewart and Jim Maxon, to incorporate a fourth stage of organizational growth which I call *community*. I first saw their model presented by Valerie at a Conference of the Association of Management Education and Development (AMED)[11] in 1988. At the time it seemed to me to stop short. Since then I have combined it with a simplified version of ego states (from transactional analysis[12]) to arrive at the diagram in Figure 2.1.

In the beginning there is one 'pioneer', perhaps an entrepreneur, perhaps a visionary, who has an idea which needs an organization for its fulfilment. This may be a new product to be manufactured and marketed, a service to be offered (such as the National Health Service) or a network to be established (such as a professional association). The originator may

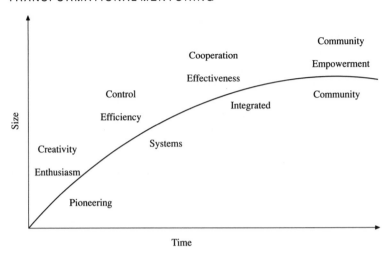

Figure 2.1   *The stages of an organization*

start alone, but will be joined by more pioneers as the organization begins to grow.

In these early stages, therefore, the organization is staffed by enthusiastic, innovative people. They tend to operate mostly from Child ego state, with all the innate energy and creativity that each real child has and which only some of us seem to retain into adulthood. Leadership seems relatively easy, with most interactions being Natural Child–Natural Child.

After a while, however, the growth leads to difficulties. Everyone is so busy being innovative that no-one is taking care of routine tasks such as getting the bills paid. Duplication starts to become a problem, and communication is no longer so easy when the numbers involved have increased.

At this stage, many organizations founder due to poor cash flow, production problems, erratic quality control or similar procedural deficiencies. Those that survive tend to do so by bringing in additional staff who have a different perspective. These new recruits are selected because they are systems-oriented. They make sure that 'proper procedures' are put in place and so add efficiency to the enthusiasm that was already there.

The systems people are characterised by their use of Parent ego state. They have experience of how things 'should be done', so they introduce rules and procedure manuals. They occupy roles as accountants or middle managers and are rewarded by the organization for taking control. Leadership now tends to focus on Controlling Parent–Adapted Child interactions. In more paternalistic organizations, it may instead be Nurturing Parent–Natural Child.

Regrettably, the organization may find, after a time, that it is facing a new crisis. The systems people become so efficient that they stifle the creativity and enthusiasm of the pioneers. When this happens, innovation ceases and the best people may even leave. Staff spend their time trying to find ways around the system, filling in forms rather than designing new products, providing statistical returns instead of spending time with customers, and so on. If a paternalistic mode has been adopted, staff feel so protected that they come to believe that the organization owes them a living. The organisation is slowly strangled by its own system.

Organizations which survive the systems crisis do so by bringing in yet another group of people. This time it is the turn of the integrators, who mediate between the pioneers and the systems people. The integrators (who may be employed in personnel, human resources or employee relations) use mainly Functional Adult ego state, relying neither on Parent experience nor Child emotion. They aim to help the managers recognize the emotional needs of the staff—and the staff to accept the wisdom and experience of the management.

This process may be helped through typical integrator-initiated activities, such as having courses in people skills, appraisal schemes, tighter selection procedures, and so on. If these are successful, the organization continues to grow because the integrators have increased the *effectiveness* with which the *efficiency* and the *enthusiasm* are combined. Leadership is now seen to need Functional Adult–Functional Adult interactions, with joint problem solving moving up the agenda.

The Stewart and Maxon model stops there. However, I believe there is more to come. If the organization remains at the integrated stage, we still have a pattern where some ego states are not in use. Often, the result is simply that it takes three people to provide a full complement of three ego states. The bulk of the workforce is still mostly in Child, the managers are still operating in Parent, and Adult is provided by the personnel department.

The organization as community

What is needed is for all individuals to recognize that they have all ego states, and to use them. *Empowerment* has become a somewhat hackneyed term, but that word captures best the approach that will be needed for the future. The organization must become a real community, where people can utilize their full capabilities. This will necessitate a significant shift from the 'one ego state per person' mode.

In Figure 2.1 I show the size of the organization at this stage to be reducing. This occurs because people intuitively sense that true community is difficult to attain with very large numbers. Gore-Tex, for example, runs very successfully with a policy of keeping unit size down to around 200 people[13]. Semco in Brazil likewise split their business units when they reach about 150 co-workers[14].

I think that the recession has masked the trend towards community because it has meant that organizations have reduced in size considerably in response to market forces. Looked at more closely, there are a number of indicators of a significant shift in the way in which people view their organizations. For example, we have Roger Harrison[15] writing on 'love in the workplace'. There has also been the general growth in the personal development market for books, tapes and workshops. In addition, the focus on equal opportunities and anti-discriminatory practices has stimulated much challenge to traditional organizational structures and processes.

Using the concept of ego states gives us another explanation for the decrease in organizational size—when we empower people we triple the number of ego states in use! Now we get the benefits of everyone's previous experience, their problem solving, their friendliness and their creativity.

It has been said that management and parenthood are the only jobs that people are expected, and allowed, to do without any training. Both have the potential to have a major impact on the lives of others! The similarities extend to the way in which we are assumed to acquire the necessary skills through osmosis because we see them going on around us. The same could often be said of mentors. Even when mentoring training is provided, it is often geared towards enabling mentors to better pass on the existing management styles.

Unfortunately, many of us do not have much contact with highly experienced managers or parents. Our own parents are usually new to the job and do much of their practising on us, learning through their mistakes as they see the results. Many times they either repeat the errors of their own parents, or over-compensate dramatically. The same process applies to management, even down to the way in which 'experts' provide advice which is subsequently contradicted by later 'experts'. Belatedly, most of us realize that employees (and babies) are individuals and need to be treated differently—although we may well be grandparents before we learn this.

Moving towards community and empowerment has significant implications for mentors. Traditional styles of *anything* will, in future, have limited usefulness if we want our organizations to be filled with employees who use initiative, make decisions, take responsibility for quality and interact well with colleagues and customers.

Notes

1. Wilson Schaef, Anne and Fassel, Diane, *The Addictive Organization*, HarperSanFrancisco, 1988.
2. Morgan, Gareth, *Images of Organization*, Sage, 1986.
3. Morgan, Gareth, *Imaginization*, Sage, 1993.
4. Bohm, D., *Wholeness and the Implicate Order*, Routledge and Kegan Paul, 1980.
5. Barham, Kevin and Rassain, Clive, Ashridge Management Research Group, *Shaping the Corporate Future*, Unwin Hyman Ltd, 1989.
6. Aburdene, Patricia and Naisbitt, John, *Megatrends for Women*, Random House, 1993.
7. Popcorn, Faith, *The Popcorn Report*, Doubleday, 1991.
8. Pedler, Mike, Burgoyne, John and Boydell, Tom, *The Learning Company*, McGraw-Hill, 1991.
9. Kirton, Michael, *Adaptors and Innovators: Cognitive Style and Personality*, Hatfield Polytechnic, 1984. Kirton Adaptation Innovation Inventory is available only to those who have completed a Certification Course. For more information, contact KAI Occupational Research Centre, Highlands, Gravel Path, Berkhamstead, Herts HP4 2PQ, UK.
10. Peck, M. Scott, *The Different Drum*, Rider & Co, 1987.
11. Stewart, Valerie and Maxon, Jim, *Management Succession During Organization Change*, paper presented by Valerie Stewart at AMED Conference, 1988.
12. For an explanation of transactional analysis concepts applied to organizations, see Hay, Julie, *Working it Out at Work–Understanding Attitudes and Building Relationships*, Sherwood, 1993.
13. See Lester, Tom, 'The Gores' Happy Family' in *Management Today*, February 1993.
14. Semler, Ricardo, *Maverick*, Century, 1993.
15. Harrison, Roger, *Organization Culture and Quality of Service: A Strategy for Releasing Love in the Workplace*, Association of Management Education and Development, 1987.

3 | Trends: The individual perspective

Some of the trends described in the previous chapter can be turned around to represent the ways in which people are changing their expectations of working life. Learning organizations may be the result or the cause of employees recognizing that there should be more to life than stagnating within an organization, especially one which no longer guarantees lifetime employment. Other trends which can be linked to an increasing concern for quality of life include such aspects as flexible working, job sharing, homeworking, telecommuting, *cashing out* and *cocooning* (two more Popcorn[1] terms).

Then there are trends related to careers—or at least to a major change in the way in which careers are viewed. Comments are made about the need to zigzag to the top; however, I doubt that the top is going to be the aim for many people. Careers are increasingly being seen as sideways movement patterns, so that we continue developing without necessarily having to be a 'leader'.

The nature of leadership is also being reworked. Current articles and books abound on the need to create teams, to become leaders of teams, or even to form self-managed cells without formal leaders. Team coaches are being substituted for managers, and we now have *gold-collar workers*[2], who will need a very different management style.

Cashing-out

A significant trend identified by Popcorn, that is particularly likely to represent change for older managers/mentors, is *cashing-out*. Cashing-out refers to the balance between living and working. She points out that the eighties was a time when people lived to work. Before that we worked to live. Now, it seems, we simply want to live—with less emphasis on money and more on quality of life.

Modern-day stress at work is high. Organizations no longer promise job security in return for hard work and company loyalty. Even competent performers are made redundant, so that people are less likely to 'give their all' to the company that may terminate their employment however hard they have worked.

A recent preliminary report of the Employment in Britain survey[3] found that only a small minority feel committed to their organization. Job security was rated third in importance, after acceptable level of pay and work they like doing. Organizational commitment was strongly related to opportunities for personal development.

Another survey of long-term employment strategies, by the Institute of Management and Manpower[4], shows that 66 per cent of the UK's organizations expect to restructure again over the next four years, even though 90 per cent of such organizations have already restructured during the last five years.

It is hardly surprising, then, that Golzen and Garner[5] suggest that employees are like professional football players, offering maximum performance to their current club but keeping an eye firmly on the transfer market. Herriot[6] gives an example of a company in the information technology (IT) sector which trains employees in IT languages they will not use, just to keep them employable elsewhere. This assures them of their continuing 'marketability'—they stay with the company as long as they are confident that they are maintaining their options to get jobs elsewhere, should this prove necessary. Barham and Rassain[7] give a similar example of Norsk Data allowing entrepreneurialism within the company, so that they retain people who might otherwise leave to set up their own businesses.

Popcorn's description of cashing-out relates mainly to the move away from high income demands into spending time in non-work pursuits like gardening and life in the country. The survey findings in the UK focus more on the reductions in levels of commitment in the aftermath of so many restructurings and redundancies. Whichever basis we start from, we still arrive at an organizational climate in which employees are no longer likely to believe that their future will involve long-term employment with the same company.

Put another way by Charles Handy (quoted by Richard Halstead in *Business Age*, May 1993), employers will need to say 'Join us and get qualified to leave us.' Handy thinks that, in any case, most people are likely to reach the end of their corporate careers by the time they are 50.

People are increasingly likely, therefore, to regard as irrelevant any mentoring which focuses on implanting specific organizational norms. Instead, they will want help to build up their portfolios. They will want to feel that the mentor is at least neutral and at best placing most emphasis on the needs of the mentee.

Popcorn writes that the question of the age in the USA seems to be 'Is this all there is?' Cashing-out means that we are opting for greater quality of life. She points out that levels of camping, gardening and other back-to-nature pursuits are rising in the USA. People need time for these activities so they are working fewer hours and are working from home more.

In the UK, however, we have a statement instead of a question—'It can't happen to me.' This is the conclusion from a recent survey reported in *Management Today*[8], which indicates that British managers are working long hours, with extra responsibilities because others have been made redundant, and with symptoms of stress—and yet they still seem to believe that their jobs are secure. Handy[9] describes this as half the people being paid twice as much for doing three times as much work, while the other half are unemployed.

It seems likely that even British managers will eventually recognize that organizational life has changed considerably, and then they, too, will start to show more concern for their quality of life.

Cocooning

Popcorn also points out a trend towards *cocooning*—a self-preservation action that means we are developing a bunker mentality as a response to the uncertainty and threat we perceive in the world. Thus, we have *armoured* cocoons, where we hire our own security services or form clubs that are closed except to those we choose to invite in. We have *wandering* cocoons, such as cars, trains and planes, where the environment is controlled and we take with us the comforts of home. Then, in our *socialized* cocoon, we restrict our contacts to close friends and family instead of entertaining for business advancement.

Cocooning and cashing-out are both trends that will fit with working patterns involving less time spent physically within the organization. Working at home, working from home, telecommuting, hot desking... technology is reinforcing, or allowing, these shifts. In turn, the trends have implications for the environment. Fewer journeys to work means less pollution, lower energy consumption and less traffic congestion for those still travelling.

People spending less time at work will not want to make an extra journey just to see a mentor. This will be another reason for not using senior managers within the organization—people will look instead for mentors who live in the same area. This will also lead to the use of mentors who are self-employed or retired.

Flexible working

Aburdene and Naisbitt[10] identify a similar change as one of the megatrends for women. Whether we see it as technology-led or as women (and some men) rejecting a format for business that conflicts with family and environmental priorities, we are likely to have more people working away from the organization in future. In a survey of long-term employment strategies, the Institute of Management[11] found that three quarters of employers expect to be using flexible working among permanent staff and to have more contracting out by 1997. Another survey[12] shows that a similar proportion of employers already employ part-time managers, although most of these are women.

The link with human growth arises when we consider how individuals will operate as these trends take increasing effect. Working away from an organization means that traditional management practices will become irrelevant. Although there may well be instant telecommunications links, people will almost certainly be making more decisions on their own. They are likely to be in tele-contact with colleagues, and directly with customers, so that they deal with a wider range of issues than might have been the case when they had a supervisor nearby. They will have to be self-motivated and disciplined—especially as they will have sufficient flexibility to choose their own working hours to fit around domestic commitments and social preferences.

They will also need to take the initiative in keeping themselves informed and up-to-date. Experienced telecommuters in California have learned to maintain their contacts and their exposure to senior management by spending some time regularly inside the organization. FI International, which was set up and became very successful specifically as an organization for people working at home, now has its homeworkers asking for centres where they can meet their colleagues. This is an indicator of the human need for contact. As more people start working alone, there will be a requirement for various forms of support. It will not just be information or companionship that people want—they will need encouragement to develop themselves and find ways of extending their skills and their quality of life.

In addition to the local mentoring described above, we could have 'mentor centres' or 'mentoring cottages'—places where people could meet for mentoring sessions and to share experiences with other mentors or mentees. A relatively public place like this could also be a sensible way of avoiding the potential risks of meeting in a home that may otherwise be unoccupied. Although there are no known cases of mentor/mentee murder, there have certainly been instances of rumours about private meetings.

Career snakes and ladders

One of the comments made about part-time working, particularly for managers, is that career prospects are put at risk. However, there are many indications that career ladders are, in any case, becoming more like a game of snakes and ladders!

There are any number of surveys and reports which show that organizations have been delayering, that they have been shedding employees at all levels and that organizational life will never be the same again. The general messages that emerge from these findings are that:

- Promotion hierarchies are disappearing as organizations become flatter.
- Organizations will continue restructuring—perhaps forever?
- People need to have broader sets of skills and experiences.
- People, including managers, should now expect to be employed in a series of organizations during their working life.
- Many people can also expect to undergo shifts between different functions, so that they end up training for several 'careers' over a period of time.
- No-one can rely on having employment until they retire.

What is even more interesting is the finding that many of the managers who are made redundant are in fact the ones with high levels of intelligence, stability, experience and problem-solving ability. In a study by Dr Mike Smith at UMIST[13] which checked out more than 200 clients of an outplacement company, it seems that it is the more venturesome and independent (and, arguably, more effective) people who are being 'invited' to leave.

It is interesting to speculate whether the same pattern applies at other levels. First-hand experience of the major redundancy programme many years ago in British Airways certainly bears this out—although it was the voluntary nature of the redundancy programme that attracted many competent people to apply for severance because they knew they could get jobs elsewhere, while many less competent employees played safe and stayed. (Note: lest my former colleagues get upset, let me stress that not everyone who stayed was incompetent—after all, I stayed put!)

This rather serendipitous manner in which careers are formed leads to three conclusions:

- We need to stop thinking of careers as something to do with moving up the hierarchy.
- We need to explore options for widening our experience so that we can move elsewhere more easily.
- If we are very competent we are likely to change jobs (often involuntarily) more often.

One group of people who are already operating on these beliefs are the interim managers. There have always been temporary staff and sub-contract staff. Now, however, there is also executive leasing as an alternative resourcing option. Described by Judith Oliver in Management Today, May 1994, this new group might be thought of as throwaway managers, who come in, sort things out and then move on. Working at a much higher level than 'temps' in the past, these freelance executives typically function at board level or just below. Oliver says they tend to be 45 or older and are generally over-qualified for the tasks they undertake. This allows them to 'hit the road running'.

Oliver does not mention whether the interim managers have mentors—probably not, since it sounds as if they work regular 12-hour days. However, the impact on mentoring for employees is clear. If senior posts are filled on a temporary basis, mentoring for employees further down the organization will not fit the traditional pattern. Even if the interim managers found the time, they would be unlikely to pass on established cultural values. Indeed, the reason for their presence may be to change these values anyway.

Gold-collar workers

Robert Kelley[14] gave us the concept of *gold-collar worker*: when he wrote of harnessing the brainpower of the workforce. Philip Sadler[2] uses the term to refer to the most talented members of the workforce. He suggests that organizations might show the value of their talented employees on the balance sheet, which is something only football clubs seem to do. Perhaps if they did they would be more careful about making employees redundant.

Sadler describes how Merck, the US drug company, attracts and develops talented people. Its methods include moving people across functions to improve their development, as well as having many multi-divisional and multi-functional task forces. It also has a two-track career path so that employees can progress for scientific or for managerial competence.

Other options used by various organizations include secondments to different functions within the same company, to other companies, and quite often to charities. There are even specialist agencies now which will organize part-time non-executive director posts in different companies for individuals whose own companies want them to acquire a wider perspective of business.

The concept of gold-collar worker appears to fit well with the notion that people need to take responsibility for initiating and maintaining their own development programmes. Talented people will do this, as they will want to reach their full potential. Organizations may provide the opportunities, but the motivation will come from the individual. This will enable them to maintain the momentum even when they are not attached to an organization—the skilled player will continue to practise and build up skills between matches.

What does not fit so well is the implication that only some of the people are talented. I am writing this at a time when people with disabilities have mounted demonstrations outside Parliament because the Bill that might have given them equal rights concerning employment opportunities was talked out. At the same time, there are letters in the personnel journals about ageism. And we still have a long way to go regarding anti-discriminatory practices generally.

The concept of gold-collar workers applied to anyone who is keen on self-development would be a better image. The star football player can't score any goals without the rest of the team. There also needs to be two teams playing together, referees and linespeople, a host of organizers and administrators to arrange fixtures, sell tickets, keep league tables, someone to mow the grass, paint the white lines, mend the nets. . . .

In Chapter 1 I mentioned *physis*—the inbuilt drive we all have to grow and develop. The trends towards cashing out and cocooning are indicators that individuals are paying more attention to their own needs and becoming less inclined to sacrifice themselves for the organization. Organizations will increasingly have to change in ways which make them healthier places to work in. Psychological health will require opportunities for all of us to be treated as gold-collar workers.

In a major comparative study by Storey *et al*[15], it was found that education and training booklets were circulated to all employees in Japanese companies. Most British organizations in the survey had not even disseminated this type of information successfully to the managers. The study showed that the Japanese treated training and development more seriously, and that they focused on general 'capability development' rather than the more restricted 'management development'. People in Japanese companies were not specifically targeted for development; instead, the Japanese emphasized continuous professional development on an ongoing basis for everyone. Japanese managers were regularly appraised against their responsibility for developing their subordinates, and were *expected* to spend time on this.

In the Employment in Britain Survey[16] reported in 1993, training opportunities were seen as more important than promotion prospects (27 per cent rated training as essential, compared to 11 per cent for promotion prospects). However, only one in five of those who wanted training actually believed that they were likely to get it. Clearly we have a long way to go in the UK to match the Japanese pattern.

We must remember also that these findings in the UK and Japan relate only to people who are/(were) in employment. It has been estimated that only one third of the working population in Japan are employed by organizations likely to figure in these surveys. The other two thirds work under very different conditions, including those in subcontract companies which enable the larger companies to deal with their workload peaks and troughs. If Handy[17] is right, the UK is fast developing a similar pattern.

There is no reason to suppose that people in the peripheral organizations, and, indeed, those who are unemployed, will be any less keen to develop themselves given the opportunity. We will therefore need innovative ways of providing gold-collar status to anyone who wants it.

Teams and leaders versus managers

Flatter organizations, flexible working and talented individuals mean that leadership styles need to change. Some organizations have already dispensed with managers, some have changed their supervisors into team leaders or coaches, and yet others have opted for self-managed teams. Each of these approaches provides opportunities for individuals to extend their responsibilities and skills.

In three successive months from January 1994, the following examples appeared in *Personnel Management*:

■ An item about a survey by Ingersoll Engineers shows that nearly three-quarters of UK engineering companies now have semi-autonomous mini-business cells in operation.
■ An article by Anat Arkin describing how supervisors became team leaders at Hickson Fine Chemicals, and how they have been identifying their own development needs and training each other, as well as handling various tasks that were previously done by plant managers.
■ An item about British Sugar eliminating the term 'foreman', giving the foremen wider roles as team coaches and facilitators, and redesignating most workers as multi-skilled technicians.

Self-managed work teams will need a different approach to leadership. Where there is less formal authority, the nature of leadership will become even more significant if teams are not to drift into confusion. The obvious 'leadership' need may be about coordination of the task, but there will also be a requirement for 'leadership' related to the process. How will the boundaries be maintained? How will team members communicate with each other? How will they develop cohesiveness, etc?

David Barry[18] suggests that self-managed teams will need *distributed* leadership. A dynamic pattern will emerge in which different people take leadership responsibility at different times for different aspects. He describes four forms of this leadership: envisioning, organizing, spanning and social. Individuals who seek to operate as members of such teams will need to develop corresponding leadership abilities.

Envisioning refers to the generation of new visions and provision or stimulation of the creative thinking needed if the team is to innovate and continue to develop new thinking. *Organizing* leadership is then needed to put the new ideas into practice and to ensure that the appropriate tasks are completed. *Spanning* leadership is about forming bridges between the team and those outside it, through activities such as networking, obtaining resources and image building. *Social* leadership refers to the group process itself, including the social, emotional and psychological levels of communication.

In self-managed groups the individuals will need to be competent at as many of these forms of leadership as possible, so that they can 'take their turn'. If they cannot do this, the team will revert to the leader/follower styles of typical hierarchies. A mentoring approach which focuses on interpersonal skills and relationship building will thus become far more relevant than one which emphasizes experience and exposure within the organization.

Team members will also need to develop ways of appraising each other. The use of peer and subordinate appraisal is being used in more and more companies, especially in the USA. In the UK, a number of organizations have started to use questionnaires, completed anonymously and collated by consultants. Some, such as American Express, are on record[19] as having used this method for some time.

This format for appraisal can be very valuable because of the high level of accuracy—people working closely together can be far more perceptive of each other's strengths and weaknesses than managers observing from a greater distance. However, this very accuracy can also lead to considerable stress, and individuals will find it helpful to have an unbiased mentor for support and challenge as they use the data.

Notes

1. Popcorn, Faith, *The Popcorn Report*, Doubleday, 1991.
2. Sadler, Philip, 'Gold Collar Workers: what makes them play their best?', *Personnel Management*, April 1994.
3. Gallie, Duncan and White, Michael, *Employee Commitment and the Skills Revolution*, PSI Publishing/Policy Studies Institute (preliminary report of Employment in Britain Survey), 1993.
4. *The Survey of Long-term Employment Strategies*, by Institute of Management and Manpower PLC, 1993 (available from the Institute of Management).
5. Golzen, Godfrey and Garner, Andrew, *Smart Moves: Successful Strategies and Tactics for Career Management*, Basil Blackwell, 1990.
6. Herriot, Peter, *The Career Management Challenge: Balancing Individual and Organisational Needs*, Sage, 1992.

7. Barham, Kevin and Rassain, Clive, Ashridge Management Research Group, *Shaping the Corporate Future*, Unwin Hyman Ltd, 1989.
8. Survey conducted by *Management Today* in conjunction with the Institute of Management–see *Management Today*, October 1993.
9. Handy, Charles, *The Empty Raincoat*, Hutchinson, 1994.
10. Aburdene, Patricia and Naisbitt, John, *Megatrends for Women*, Random House, 1993.
11. *The Survey of Long Term Employment Strategies*, Institute of Management, 1993.
12. Boyer, Isabel, *Flexible Working for Managers*, Chartered Institute of Management Accountants, 1993.
13. Quoted in Charleworth, Paul, 'Don't Lose your Valuable Staff', in *Professional Manager*, May 1994.
14. Kelley, Robert E., 'The Gold-Collar Worker: Harnessing the Brainpower of the New Work Force', quoted in *Strategy of the Dolphin* by Dudley Lynch and Paul L. Kordis, Arrow Books, 1988.
15. Storey, John, Okasaki-Ward, Lola, Sisson, Keith, *et al*, *Managers and Management Development in Britain and Japan*, Basil Blackwell, 1992.
16. Gallie, Duncan and White, Michael, *Employee Commitment and the Skills Revolution*, PSI Publishing/Policy Studies Institute (preliminary report of Employment in Britain Survey), 1993.
17. Handy, Charles, *The Age of Unreason*, Business Books Ltd, 1989.
18. Barry, Dr David, 'Managing the Bossless Team: Lessons in Distributed Leadership', in *Organizational Dynamics*, Summer 1991, pages 31–47.
19. Fletcher, Clive, *Appraisal: Routes to Improved Performance*, IPM, 1993.

4 | What happens now?

What gets called 'mentoring'?

Although I have referred to traditional mentoring as if it is a distinct and well-known approach, the real situation is far more complicated. The range of activities called 'mentoring' is very wide—ask someone what mentoring is and they may say:

- Showing people the ropes—and helping them to climb them
- Passing on knowledge and/or skills, formally or informally
- Looking after people
- Acting as a sounding board
- Helping people to put learning into practice
- Being a role model
- Being a guide
- Being a champion
- Talking to people about their careers
- Counselling
- Coaching.

You may well be able to add others! I also found that there were many different jobs where mentoring seemed to be included. Although some people believed firmly that mentoring was the responsibility of managers, others said lots of people acted as mentors as part of what they were doing. Examples included:

> personnel officers, training officers, facilitators, consultants, trade union officers, staff representatives, nursing and other medical staff, teachers, counsellors, sports coaches, supervisors, team leaders, probation officers, social workers, therapists, outplacement counsellors, career counsellors, small business advisers, BS 5750 consultants and assessors, action learning set members, welfare staff . . .

Many of these responses are based on the traditional model of mentoring, with one person passing on their greater wisdom and experience to another. However, others confuse mentoring with other methods, such as coaching or counselling. I think all of these functions are necessary and important—but they are not all mentoring in the original sense of the word.

Who was Mentor?

Most books on mentoring tell us about Mentor, so I will keep this brief. He was the Greek god who was asked by Ulysses to take care of his son, Telemachus, while Ulysses himself went off on his travels. Mentor therefore brought up Telemachus, acting rather like an uncle. In the way of most Greek gods, Mentor had an alias—he was otherwise known as Athena, the warlike goddess of wisdom and protector of craftsmen. In either case, whether as Mentor or Athena, the arrangement was that of an older, wiser person taking overall charge of a younger, less experienced protégé.

Mentor thus gave his name to the traditional mentoring arrangements, from the time of apprentices who served with master craftsmen, through to the senior manager/high flyer arrangements which exist in many organizations. Although this no longer carries the opportunity to marry the craftsman's daughter and inherit the firm, it may well involve the mentor in creating opportunities for the protégé to carry out particular projects or tasks, seeing that other senior managers realize how competent the protégé is, and even organizing promotions for the protégé. This is great if you are selected as a high flyer, but not so good if you are not. Those outside the scheme tend to see it as nepotism and favouritism.

Mentoring formats

I am suggesting in this book that we replace the traditional and other forms of mentoring with developmental alliances. For you to consider this, you need to know what these existing approaches are. In some very traditional organizations it may even be necessary to establish one of the other mentoring formats first, to pave the way.

I visited a number of organizations, read a number of books (mentoring is a growth area in the literature!) and talked to a lot of people. As I mentioned earlier, I found a myriad of activities that were called mentoring. I have classified these into several broad groups:

- Those that come closest to the traditional older/younger pattern
- Those that are part of training and development processes
- Those that have an expert/novice connotation
- Those that are based on the principle of friend or comrade
- Those that operate on a temporary deficit model
- *Ad hoc* arrangements
- Those that don't exist!

The last group is for those organizations where there is no obvious mentoring activity. These include some where mentoring has been considered but no action has resulted: 'We are very interested in mentoring. A report went to senior management a couple of years ago but we are still waiting for a decision.'

Older/Younger

This model of mentoring is the one which David Clutterbuck[1] describes so well. It is also the only approach for which the 'mentor' label is accurate—mentors in this case are generally older and hopefully wiser and do act like Mentor with Telemachus (although I'm not sure who or where Ulysses is).

The older/younger pattern includes programmes such as the well-known Civil Service high-flyer scheme for administrative trainees. This format is used particularly in organizations which are still firmly hierarchical. These schemes are usually fairly formalized, with sets of procedures to cover most aspects. There will typically be established criteria against which mentees are selected for places on the scheme. However, the manager often has the final say in who will be a mentee, so there is a need to behave as required in order to be chosen. There may also be training programmes for mentors and a procedure for matching mentor to mentee.

The role of the mentor will include advising the protégé on what is expected by the organization. Mentors may let mentees know of possible development opportunities, such as assignments, projects or training courses. They will also help the protégé to understand the 'politics' of the organization.

Roffey Park have described in several of their newsletters how the GKN mentoring scheme has been developed along these lines. The mentor will already be a successful manager, in a senior, influential position, with enough authority to help the mentee obtain the resources needed. The aim is to give younger managers the experience they need to move around within the organization.

In some traditional schemes, mentors are regarded as sponsors and play an active part in finding developmental or promotional opportunities for the protégé. They are also likely to represent the mentee's interests to senior management. A sponsor may arrange specific projects for the protégé, both as learning opportunities and as a showcase within which the protégé's talents can be displayed to others.

These traditional schemes usually require the mentors to have a good understanding of the organization and of the types of work done there. They must be able to assess the performance of the protégé and judge potential against future options. This will include knowing about the work of the protégé's immediate manager, both as a possible avenue for promotion and as a factor affecting the current situation.

Mentors in traditional schemes tend to have protégés who are expected to move around, gaining experience through a series of postings. These mentors therefore need skills in helping mentees to make choices about which postings to take and how to handle the natural stresses of frequent job and home moves. They may also have to help mentees to deal with the impact of such moves on partners and families. This is an area where mentors must balance their commitments to the needs of the organization against the best interests of the individual mentee.

The more formal schemes may also involve support from the personnel department. The aim will be to help both mentor and mentee to operate effectively. Thus, training may be provided for mentors (and, less often, for mentees) in how to make the relationship as productive as possible. Personnel may, in addition, have their own part in the process, such as when personnel officers talk directly to employees about future career prospects and development needs.

There are a number of drawbacks to the traditional mentoring format. Particularly critical has been the way in which so many organizations have been reducing the number of employees and the number of levels in the hierarchy—the so-called downsizing and outsourcing. There has, of course, been a corresponding reduction in the number of managers. This has had two effects: people are now expected, and required, to show more initiative and we have fewer managers available to act as mentors.

At the same time, our expectations about work are changing. First, we are generally better educated than previous generations. This means that we expect, and want, to be allowed to use our initiative. Second, we can see for ourselves that there are fewer opportunities available for promotion. If we want to learn and develop, we will have to find new ways to do so; we can no longer rely on moving up the levels of the hierarchy. Third, we can see for ourselves that many managers went through very different career paths to those that will apply in future—so how can they advise us when the organizational world is now so different?

Training and development

Probably the second most commonly found mentoring schemes are those that are part of training and development processes. In these cases, it is usually a tutor or trainer who is the mentor. The mentees may be the entire group on a course, or selected individuals. The Open University pattern of tutorials belongs in this category. So also do tutors and assessors who provide guidance for people seeking accreditation of prior learning (APL).

Many of us who have attended training programmes will have seen that mentoring was included as part of the course. Sometimes this may extend more into counselling, sometimes it may be restricted to coaching—but often the focus will be on helping the student to relate the training course content to application in the workplace. Much of this is done on a one-to-one basis, although a similar process on team-building courses is really mentoring of a group.

Adrian Spooner[2] defines mentors as 'the catalyst in the training reaction'; he also comments that mentors are in the best position to evaluate the training they have been supporting. In his view, the mentor 'provides the human support that trainees need if they are to interact effectively with the training system'.

There is a mentoring function for managers that also fits under the training/development label. This is the briefing and debriefing process which many organizations expect managers to undertake whenever one of their subordinates attends a course. In an ideal world, all managers would do this automatically. However, in many cases this form of mentoring is overlooked even when the requirement is clearly publicized. When such mentoring does take place, the benefits to the student, the organization, and the training course itself are noticeable.

A slightly different example is in an organization which provides training programmes for overseas students. Here the trainers expect to become involved in many aspects of the visit to the host country. In addition to the normal interest in training needs analysis and action planning, these trainers concern themselves with the students' temporary culture change. In the past the role was described by the trainers as 'nannying'. However, this feeling has disappeared, as trainers have recognized that learning will occur more readily if students are not left to struggle alone with the effects of being in a foreign country while they are on the course. The trainers will therefore assist as necessary with problems about accommodation, food, money, contact with home and so on.

A more work-focused approach occurs with programmes such as that run by the Institute of Management (formerly known as the BIM). Its Competent Manager Programme includes provision for support from a mentor, who is ideally a line manager from the student's organisation. In the 1992 training programme brochure is the comment that this provides '... help and guidance from an experienced professional while the organization benefits from training aligned to its culture and expectations'. The Institute operates a panel of mentors for those organizations where a suitable manager is not available. It also provides a three-day mentoring training course, '... backed up by a continued programme to enable mentors to provide tutorial support and guidance'.

Leeds Metropolitan University[3] take a similar stance, with a project focused on 'the role of the workplace mentor in the context of work-based learning, on their training needs and the accreditation of that learning'. For this project they define a mentor as 'the person who helps another to learn from their work practice' and state that it requires a balance of focus between educative, supportive and managerial.

The perfect group also asks whether readers agree with its view of the role of a mentor, which it suggests includes: ideas generator, supporter, guide, appraiser, friend, someone to relate to, counsellor, ally, trainer, educator/teacher, line manager, recorder and supervisor. Quite a range! And if that is not enough, in its proposed person specification for a mentor it lists previous experience and subject knowledge as essential requirements, with desirable characteristics including professional practice, organization and culture, experiential learning theory, groupwork and counselling skills, training and educational skills, plus a range of interpersonal skills—not forgetting, of course, mentoring skills.

There is another rapidly growing area under this T&D heading—the mentors associated with Scottish/National Vocational Qualifications (S/NVQs). I do not intend to join in the arguments about whether these have been hijacked by the educational establishments or overlooked by industry. However, what is clear is that S/NVQs have generated an increasing need for assessors (mentors) who help people to prepare portfolios of evidence to show their competence.

Expert/Novice

The expert/novice connotation is another theme in many mentoring activities. It can also be the main objective. The most obvious example is the master/apprentice relationship. Although apprentices may now be called trainees, and may spend more time than previously on off-the-job training, the fundamental approach is still that of an expert passing on skills. There may also be a strong emphasis on the values of the profession or trade.

The same method is applied in mentoring schemes operated by professional associations such as the Institution of Electrical Engineers. To obtain chartered status, graduates must undergo a period of mentored development in the workplace. A similar in-house format is Heads of Profession within the Civil Service. These are the senior professionals who set the pattern for others in the same profession. They set the professional or technical standards for people actually reporting to line managers who are administrators or who have a different professional background.

Many psychotherapy associations operate expert/novice arrangements. For instance, the Institute for Transactional Analysis is part of an international certification process where trainee analysts are required to have 'supervision' from an advanced member. This supervision consists of a range of options as appropriate, including teaching, questioning, challenging and supporting. The objective is to help the trainees develop the necessary self-awareness and skills so that they can become as effective therapists as their supervisors.

A slightly different focus here is the link between mentoring and coaching. The terms are often used interchangeably—Susan Bloch[4] even defines a mentor as 'a confidential coach and sounding board ...' Roffey Park, in their Autumn 1992 newsletter, were offering seminars covering mentoring and coaching as if they were the same topics.

Friend/Comrade

Mentoring schemes based on the friend or comrade model come closest to the developmental alliance approach suggested in this book. However, they still tend to be 'organized' rather than left to individuals to initiate. Corporate training departments are often the source of such an approach, setting up support networks which enable former course participants to help each other. Although this mode of mentoring is linked to training and development processes, the distinguishing factor is the emphasis on support from colleagues rather than from professional developers.

One of the major banks has a *buddies* system, with the purpose of encouraging participants to follow through on their development goals. Course members are first paired with a fellow participant so that they can learn how to set up their own guidelines about the relationship. They also practise helping processes such as listening, reflecting and so on. They are then urged to establish a similar relationship with someone more accessible once they return to the workplace.

Action learning operates in much the same way. Action learning typically involves a group of people who help each other as they undertake tasks and projects. They may be working together as a group or separately as individuals. They form a *set* and have regular meetings at which they act as supporters, challengers and teachers to each other. Many sets continue to function as support groups once the formal training programme has ceased. Increasingly, action learning sets have become a format for obtaining qualifications, such as MBAs awarded by several universities. Action learning sets have also been established specifically for longer-term support, such as one for chief executives of local authorities where typical content relates to the current issues of those attending. In a report on 'Developing the Developers' prepared for the Association of Management Education and Development (AMED) by Tom Boydell in 1991, AMED was advised to offer a mentoring service which might use learning sets and support groups.

Some employee assistance programmes (EAPs) also rely on collegial support. British Airways has an EAP operated by volunteer counsellors, who are given training and supervision by professionals but who then help their colleagues to resolve problems. Where the issues raised relate to career and development prospects, the volunteers are acting as mentors when they use their skills to help the counsellees to clarify the situation and consider their options.

Temporary deficit

The temporary deficit model covers those approaches where the mentee is seen to need only short-term support. A government agency uses the term 'mentoring' to cover a scheme whereby new area managers 'shadow' more experienced area managers until they have acquired enough experience and knowledge to take up a substantive appointment. This approach is used because there are too few new appointments annually to justify mounting a training programme.

A retail organization has another version: it allocates new department managers to mentors who are already department managers but in different stores. The new managers operate for three or four months *without portfolio*—they are based in a store, but have regular contact with their mentors as they learn the job. It is felt that the new managers find it easier to ask for guidance from colleagues than from the store managers to whom they report. It is also believed that department managers understand detailed aspects of the role better than store managers do.

Many temporary deficit models often sound rather like the old 'sitting by Nellie' approach to training. An inexperienced employee is paired with an experienced person for the purpose of learning the job. The usual mentoring focus on future development may well be restricted to a future of only a few weeks.

Ad hoc

Finally we come to the *ad hoc* arrangements. This category includes a variety of arrangements initiated by mentees, together with examples of people who realized later that they had been heavily influenced by particular individuals in the past. Biographies of captains of industry often carry quotes about the influence of specific individuals, especially those who made profound comments in memorable language.

Other examples include many women who recognize that they were mentored at some stage of their careers on an informal basis by senior, male managers. An increasing number report being mentored by women who had already reached senior positions. However, there are still accounts of senior women who seem reluctant to help other women follow them up the ladder. Yet others talk of finding their own mentors from elsewhere. A common route seems to be through the variety of women's networks which now exist. There are also instances of friends and colleagues operating as mentors on an *ad ho*c basis, as when an outplacement counsellor used his skills without payment to help a friend determine a more appropriate career direction.

Ad hoc arrangements also include role reversals, when the subordinate acts as mentor to the manager. This occurs when the manager is newly appointed and has experienced staff. It requires a high level of trust and openness. When this can be achieved, there are many benefits. The manager gains from the challenge and the provision of good information about the work. The subordinate gains in confidence and motivation, learns the skills of giving constructive feedback, and becomes even more committed to the success of the section.

Wouldn't Janus have been better than Mentor?

I have continued to use the term *'mentoring'* although I am proposing a significantly different approach—mainly because I have been unable to find a better alternative. It would have been nice if Mentor's female form, Athena, could have been the role model for a different style of mentoring, away from the stereotypical male culture. Regrettably, this seems unlikely. Athena may well have befriended and helped various heroes, but she did so in a very 'unfeminine' way. Although her epithets include *Pronoia* (the Foreseeing) and *Boulaia* (the Counsellor-goddess), she is also credited with killing Pallas, Enceladus and Ares and turning Arachne into a spider.

I did consider for a while whether to use Janus, who was the Roman god of doors, openings and beginnings. He opened the doors for others to walk through. This seemed to me to be a far more appropriate style for today's world of constant change and increased self-reliance. Unfortunately, Janus also seems to have a persona that involves being two-faced—another drawback if the term *'janitor'* were not enough to rule him out.

However, the Janus style captures better the underlying value which I associate with a developmental alliance:

- Growth and development are natural human drives.
- We are all capable of taking charge of our own development.
- We are capable of helping other people to think through and make their own decisions.

Golzen and Garner[5], writing about career management, suggest that *'In a career sense we are all self-employed now'*. For me, this captures the essence of the changes that are happening in organizations and that will overtake traditional mentoring schemes. Each of us needs to take responsibility for our own development rather than relying on 'the organization', or a mentor, to look after us. At the same time we are also expected to engage in continuous professional development, play our part in learning organizations, take responsibility for environmental stewardship, implement liberation management and do all of this within a context of organizational transformation. So we need a colleague who is also a friend, who will support and challenge, in order for us to come to our own conclusions and make our own decisions.

Notes

1. Clutterbuck, David, *Everyone Needs a Mentor*, IPM, 2nd edn, 1991.
2. Spooner, Adrian, 'Mentoring and Flexible Training', in *Management Development Review*, Vol. 6, No. 2, 1993, pages 21-5.
3. Leeds Metropolitan University issued a newsletter entitled *Mentoring–The 'Working for a Degree'Pproject*. This project concluded with a conference in September 1994.
4. Bloch, Susan, 'Business Mentoring and Coaching', in *Training and Development*, April 1993.
5. Golzen, Godfrey and Garner, Andrew, *Smart Moves: Successful Strategies and Tactics for Career Management*, Basil Blackwell, 1990.

Checklist: What happens in your organization?

You might now like to revisit the questions at the end of Chapter 1. You can extend your responses to take account of the different mentoring formats.

Which of the following approaches are in existence? How are they organized? Who is involved in them? What are the advantages and drawbacks?

- Older/younger—e.g. traditional, formal schemes for high flyers
- Training and development—e.g. related to training programmes, further education, S/NVQs
- Expert/novice—e.g. professional specialists monitoring the development of junior colleagues
- Friend/comrade—e.g. support groups
- Temporary deficit—e.g. short-term 'minders'
- *Ad hoc*—e.g. individual arrangements.

How close do your mentoring arrangements come to the *Janus* model?

5 What is a developmental alliance?

A definition

Let me start by restating the definition I gave in Chapter 1, to save you turning back.

> a relationship between equals in which one or more of those involved is enabled to
>
> increase awareness,
> identify alternatives and
> initiate action
>
> to develop themselves

I've already pointed out the significance of *equals*. Several other words are also carefully selected.

Developmental alliance

I put these two words together to emphasize that the two concepts are combined—that it is development through the process of an alliance, and an alliance for the specific purpose of development.

Development refers to an approach that covers long-term, significant growth rather than short-term, short-focus problem solving. It relates to the whole person, in work and personal life, in career and personal growth, and the ways in which they balance these diverse elements.

Alliance indicates that the approach involves two (or more) people coming together for a common purpose. It also implies that they will agree how they will function together. They will have a 'treaty', or contract, with rules and boundaries that each party finds acceptable and useful.

Relationship

Relationship is used to make the point that people engaged in this approach make a real connection with each other. Discussion of long-term growth requires a high level of trust in both directions. The mentee needs to feel able to share their concerns and discuss their weaknesses; the mentor needs to be able to do the same when this might help the mentee. There will also be times when neither party is sure what to do next—they will need a strong enough human connection to admit this and work together to find a solution.

We also need a relationship in which we can celebrate successes. It is depressing if we focus only on what still has to be changed or achieved. We need an atmosphere that allows the mentee to 'boast' about achievements and the mentor to accept a share of the credit for having helped the mentee work out what to do and how to do it.

Finally, our relationship must be strong enough to survive challenges. There will be times when a mentor has to confront a mentee. Perhaps the mentee is not being logical, or is overlooking opportunities, or blaming others. The mentor needs to feel that the bond is strong enough for this to be pointed out, without any serious risk that the mentee will become defensive or withdraw from the mentoring arrangement.

I mentioned in Chapter 1 that the Gestalt approach is relevant here. Gestalt counsellors work on the premise that people can learn about themselves through the process of relating to another person—in this case, the counsellor. The key to healing is in the I-You relationship, which allows counsellor and client to explore how the client connects with others, as well as how the latter makes sense of the world. The counsellor is careful to respect the client's perceptions and not to impose personal assumptions.

Training as a Gestalt counsellor is obviously a lengthy process, and I am not suggesting that mentors must do this. I am proposing that they use the process, so that a mentor in a developmental alliance will:

- set aside their own view of the world
- use cooperative enquiry to help the mentee explore *their* world
- be fully with the mentee during this process
- be willing to review personal behaviour as a source of insight for the mentee
- be prepared to experiment with new ways of relating so that the mentee can see what happens.

Equals

Equals is there to differentiate a developmental alliance clearly from mentor/protégé, helper/client models, and because hierarchical arrangements will no longer be appropriate!

In my definition I have deliberately not said whether one party is older, or wiser, than the other. The crux will be that they are operating as equals. One of them may well be older, or wiser, or more senior, but that should not be an essential part of the arrangement. Indeed, we may need to separate out the effect of such differences so that our mentoring process is not 'contaminated'. Otherwise there is a risk that the junior partner in the arrangement will be influenced too much by the wishes of the mentor.

Another factor is that junior people with the right skills can make excellent mentors in their own right. We lose this valuable source of talent if we restrict ourselves to senior/junior pairings. The keys to successful development nowadays will instead be the ways in which we manage to act together and the skills we are able to use.

The stages of an alliance

Mentoring is similar in some ways to counselling, coaching and problem solving. However, it is also different—it needs more analysis than might occur in a counselling session, a broader perspective than for coaching and no shared responsibility as might happen with problem solving. The stages involved, therefore, are:

- alliance
- assessment
- analysis
- alternatives
- action planning
- application
- appraisal

These stages can apply at two levels or over two time periods. They are the overall stages which might be worked through over a typical mentoring life cycle lasting between 18 and 24 months. They are also applicable as a framework for *each* session.

The following is intended as an overview of the different stages. Later chapters will contain checklists and more detailed suggestions for each phase.

Stage 1: Alliance

During this stage mentor and mentee build an initial relationship. They get to know each other and create a bond, establish what the mentee hopes to gain from the mentoring, and confirm what the mentor has to offer. They jointly agree *mentoring contracts*: a general one to cover their long-term association and a specific one related to the current session.

Stage 2: Assessment

Now the mentor helps the mentee to review and describe their current situation and how they would like things to be in the future. This will include thinking about the mentee's range of skills, knowledge and experience, the organizational context in which they must work and any other aspects which might affect self-development.

Stage 3: Analysis

Next, the mentor and mentee work together to apply appropriate frameworks and theories so that the mentee gains awareness and understanding. The aim of this stage is to enable the mentee to identify what part they play in events and to recognize any trends or patterns of behaviour that are relevant.

Stage 4: Alternatives

Mentor and mentee go on to identify options which will extend the range of possibilities for the mentee. This might include ideas for development activities, consideration of different career paths, perhaps even a totally new way of looking at the world. The mentor may well function as 'devil's advocate' and challenge the mentee to take a different perspective. The relative merits of the various options are compared so that the mentee can choose and plan appropriate actions.

Stage 5: Action planning

The mentor helps the mentee to consider the implications of each option, select the best and work out a detailed action plan.

Stage 6: Application

The mentee puts the action plan into practice. This is not so much a part of the mentoring process as a result. The intended aim is that the mentee attains a greater level of autonomy, the elements of which are:

- *awareness*: understanding what is going on in the here and now, not reacting in ways which are leftovers from the past
- *alternatives*: having choices about what you might do in any situation, not feeling compelled to act in a particular way
- *authenticity*: being able to make genuine contact with other people, not hiding your reactions inappropriately.

Stage 7: Appraisal

Reviewing actions and results to check that outcomes are consistent with the personal and professional development of the mentee. This stage may be undertaken by the mentee alone or as part of subsequent interactions with the mentor. Once a mentoring relationship has been established, appraisal should become a regular feature.

As I have already pointed out, these stages apply over a period of time. It may take several sessions to form an alliance or to assess the situation. The stages may also apply as a complete sequence for each separate session. This will depend on the nature of the contract for a session. If the contract calls for an outcome from the session, there will be a need to work through to the action stage. For instance, a contract for the mentor to help the mentee to make an urgent decision on whether to accept a promotion might well mean:

- assessing the situation and the opportunity
- analysing how it fits into the overall career plan
- exploring alternatives such as rejecting it, accepting it, looking elsewhere
- deciding what action to take
- checking that the final choice supports mentee autonomy
- appraising to make sure that the decision taken is in line with the mentee's overall development plans.

Spot mentoring

So far, I have written as if the mentoring relationship is fairly long term. In formal, traditional mentoring schemes, such associations typically last up to two years—a developmental alliance is likely to need a similar length of commitment. However, the description above of a single session shows that it is also possible to have *spot mentoring*. By this I mean much shorter mentoring relationships which are set up for specific, restricted purposes. For example, a mentee might spend time with someone who has specialist experience in an area in which they would like to work. Or the mentee might seek out a colleague who has particular skills which they want to acquire.

In such cases, the mentee might ask the other person for a single session only. There would still be a 'main mentor'; the spot mentoring would be supplementary. It would be up to the mentee to make sure that the contract was clear. Whoever was asked to provide spot mentoring would need to know the purpose and limits of this interaction with the mentee, who would typically have to explain that this was part of a wider initiative for self-development. The mentee would also need to be more active in shaping how the session was run. The spot mentor may have a traditional view of mentoring—in that case the mentee would have to be very explicit about the way in which they would like the mentor to help.

The regular mentor would then be available to help the mentee to fit the spot mentoring into the wider context of the overall development planning. Say, for example, that the mentee approaches a senior manager and learns that some extra skills would be needed to work in that manager's department. The mentee may also be told how to get such skills. In the next session with the regular mentor, the mentee can consider how such activities can be fitted into the existing action plan.

There may even be a circular process. The mentee may have decided to seek spot mentoring as part of an action plan drawn up in discussion with the regular mentor. Having done so, the mentee brings the results back for review. This may help the mentee to identify the need for more or different spot mentoring. And so the process may continue, with the regular mentor being the one who helps the mentee to pull the strands together into a coherent development strategy.

Group mentoring

The same developmental alliance process can be used with groups. In this case, the mentor may be an 'external' facilitator, or one or more members of the group itself. It is possible for the entire group to be a sort of 'group mentor' to an individual within the group. However, it will probably flow better if someone is appointed as a nominal chairperson. The mentor(s) may work with an individual mentee or with several, or all, of the group. As with the one-to-one alliance, the stages may occupy a single session only or be spread over a period of time.

This style of operating is somewhat similar to that used for 'supervision' for professionals such as social workers or probation officers. The word 'supervision' is used here in a very different way from its common meaning in industry. There it means telling someone less senior what to do, whereas in social work it refers to a process whereby professionals review their caseload by discussing it with a colleague or manager. The focus is on increasing self-awareness and identifying new options for the future, rather than monitoring and checking performance levels. Such an approach can also be applied in action learning sets and support groups.

The alliance stage, as with the one-to-one version, involves building a relationship. A good connection is needed between group members so that they will feel comfortable sharing (and hearing) potentially sensitive information. If there is to be a formal facilitator, the facilitator, the mentee and the group will have to agree a three-way contract (see Chapter 6 for more details about three-cornered contracting). Even with another group member acting as the mentor, it may still be necessary to have a three-way contract which reflects the different roles and responsibilities during the mentoring process.

The assessment and analysis stages can be led by mentor and mentee, with other group members observing while thinking of their own responses related to their own situations (i.e not second-guessing the mentee). The rest of the group can also join in with questions and suggestions which will help the mentee with her or his own thinking. Sharing their own reactions may also stimulate new thinking for the mentee.

Then, in the alternatives and action planning stages, the group members can reinforce the devil's advocacy of the mentor. Several heads really are better than one (or two)! If they are knowledgeable about the circumstances, group members may also be able to point out potential pitfalls and propose ways for the mentee to increase the likelihood of successful implementation.

Finally, the group forms a ready-made support network for the application stage. This will be particularly effective if several group members are individually implementing action plans. It will also work well if there are shared concerns and related activities. Making a public pledge to action plans and having a supportive group atmosphere are key ways of reinforcing the commitment of mentees to carrying out their stated intentions.

Values and beliefs

In Chapter 1 I mentioned briefly some of the values underlying the developmental alliance approach. I will now expand on some key aspects.

People are OK

Or I could have put 'I'm OK, You're OK'[1]. This book title from the sixties has entered the language as a quick way of affirming that human beings are basically of value, that we all have needs, that we need to meet those needs in ways which do not deny the needs of others, and that if you scratch the surface of even the most obnoxious of people you will eventually get through to an inner core of human-ness.

Such a belief is essential if we are to create developmental alliances— otherwise why would we bother? Perhaps, more significantly, it is this belief that will prompt us to extend the benefits of alliances to a wider range of individuals. If we operate on the premise that *all* people are OK, there is no justification for restricting mentoring to a chosen few.

This belief also has an impact in reverse. Once we believe that we, too, are OK, then we, too, can be mentors. There is no justification for restricting the role of mentor to the chosen few! It has been established that counsellors are effective because they genuinely care about people, regardless of the theoretical base from which they work. In the same way, mentors are effective because they care about people and not because of their level within the hierarchy.

People want closeness

I mentioned in Chapter 2 that the notion of community is becoming more important in organizations; I also quoted Scott Peck[2] and other writers who are identifying the ways we are shifting towards working together rather than as individuals.

It seems to me that attachment and bonding with other people is a basic human need. It has been discouraged for many years—the Industrial Revolution, for example, wanted workers who would leave their communities, their villages or family farms and instead spend many hours isolated at workstations on production lines.

Now, as we reassert our rights to a psychologically healthy way of spending our working hours, we are rediscovering the pleasure of being in genuine contact with other human beings. As I mentioned earlier, even the employees of the FI Group, which was set up specifically for IT professionals wanting to work at home, have now asked their founder, Steve Shirley OBE, to set up neighbourhood work centres so that they can work in teams.[3]

A developmental alliance is a way of being close to another person— indeed, it depends on genuine connection. Because it is peer-based, it is also clear that mentor and mentee are coming together because they *choose* to do so and not simply because the organization expects it of them. Conversely, a developmental alliance will not work properly unless those involved believe that it is normal for people to want a close connection with each other.

People can change

I was shocked when I discovered that some trainers did not believe that people really change. However, it did bring it home to me that this is a belief and not a law of the universe—or at least it's only my belief that it is a law of the universe!

Therefore this needs to appear on the list of beliefs held by anyone who seeks to be a mentor or a mentee. I have spent the last 20 years engaged in an ongoing professional training aimed at equipping me to help other people to change, with an explicit expectation that I, too, would change considerably as I underwent the training. It may well be that our innate preferences do not change; it may be that our preferences are not innate but are programmed as we grow up. However, whether we opt to attribute our character to nature or nurture, we can still make significant changes to our patterns of behaviour. This is why mentoring can benefit us—it gives us an opportunity to examine these patterns and identify alternative options for the future.

People want to grow

Whether we accept the existence of *physis* or not (see Chapter 1), we can still see much evidence around us of the ways in which people develop over time. Many organizations have discovered the benefits of encouraging people to learn in areas not directly related to their work. There are also plenty of examples of the ways in which employees respond to the chance to join quality circles. With the right organizational environment, people show levels of initiative and creativity that they were previously not considered capable of.

There would be little point in mentoring someone if we, and they, did not believe that they could grow. We will also be better mentors if we are aware that we, too, are growing through the process of being a mentor.

We create our own meaning

This belief that we create our own meaning leads us to respect the frame of reference of the other person. Rather like my comments above about whether people change or not, we need to recognize that there are no universal laws governing people-functioning. Indeed, even in the inanimate world, scientists continue to discover that scientific laws have to be updated from time to time.

We each have our own version of reality, which we create based on our own patterns of constructs. If you doubt this, try conducting a few repertory grid interviews[4]. As you 'ladder down' someone else's constructs by asking them what evidence they base their conclusions on, you are likely to hear some surprising responses.

I recall as an example the construct 'integrity', which meant, to different people, the following: showing up for work on time every day; never being known to tell a lie; and holding steadfastly to a point of view. Others might have labelled these respectively as punctual, honest and dogmatic! For them, integrity may have yet another meaning.

It is essential, therefore, that mentors (and mentees) accept that there are many ways of interpreting the same world. It may not even be the same world if our constructs are very different. American Indians used to say that you had to walk for a day in another person's moccasins before you could understand their point of view. This is appropriate advice for anyone wanting to form a developmental alliance.

We can make decisions

That we can make decisions is a key belief if we are to move away from a 'mentor knows best' mentality. A developmental alliance between equals means that it is unacceptable and inappropriate for mentors to make choices on behalf of mentees. We must therefore believe that mentees are capable of making their own decisions.

It is interesting that people who run homes and families, and have hobbies that often require high levels of knowledge and skills, may still be seen as incapable when it comes to decision making at work. Similarly, employees who make critical decisions concerning customers, or who operate and maintain complex equipment, or who supervise the work of others, may still be considered to need much direction when they consider their future development.

It may well be true that we made poor decisions as children and thereby took on self-limiting beliefs and even an unhelpful 'lifescript'[5]. However, that was largely because we lacked information—as youngsters we generally had to rely on the grown-ups to explain the workings of the world to us. As we grew older, we may or may not have updated our information and changed our earlier decisions.

However, now that we are adults we have access to far more data. We may need prompting to check out our sources of data, but we can certainly make more informed decisions than when we were small. The role of the mentor, therefore, may be to stimulate us to check our data and our decision-making process, but it is not to make the decisions for us.

Our behaviour is purposeful

Human beings often appear to take actions which seem illogical. Sometimes the action only seems illogical because the person observing it has a different frame of reference—they are creating their own meaning instead of understanding ours. At other times, however, the behaviour really is illogical; that is, it appears to be illogical to *most* observers, including the well-known 'person in the street'.

Mentors need to recognize that all behaviour, however illogical it seems, has a purpose. Uncover the purpose and the mentee will be able to identify alternative actions for achieving the goal.

Keeping this belief in mind is also important for maintaining a developmental alliance in the face of apparently negative behaviour on the part of the mentee. For example, there may well be times when a mentor feels that the mentee is resisting the mentoring process itself, or had behaved inappropriately between mentoring sessions. When this happens, the mentor needs to keep in mind that we all do strange things when under stress. However odd our actions may seem to others, within ourselves we will feel that we had no choice if we were to achieve our objective.

Think about what happens when we talk to foreigners and cannot make ourselves understood. Most of us simply do more of the same—we talk more loudly. This is totally illogical—if they do not know our language why should they start to understand it simply because we have turned up the volume! This endearing human trait of doing more energetically anything that is not working for us is repeated in many settings. Thus, we tend to argue more fiercely with someone who will not agree with us, even though an impartial observer can see that we are, in fact, making the rift even bigger.

It is easy to forget that such adverse behaviour is really our best attempt to establish a connection with another human being. To engage in a developmental alliance, we need a firm belief about the basic purposefulness of human beings and a large degree of tolerance for the ways in which people unwittingly disguise their good intentions. Let's hope our partners in an alliance extend the same forbearance towards us.

Notes

1. *I'm OK, You're OK*, Thomas Harris, Pan, 1973. It was a best-seller and is still readily available in bookstores.
2. Peck, M. Scott, *The Different Drum*, Rider, 1987.
3. Steve Shirley is quoted by A. Forrest and P. Tolfree in *Leaders: The Learning Curve of Achievement*, Industrial Society, 1992.
4. The repertory grid is described in Bannister, D. and Fransella, F., *Inquiring Man: The Theory of Personal Constructs*, Penguin, 1971. Another useful explanation, with an organizational context, is given in Stewart, A. and Stewart, R., *Tomorrow's Men Today*, IPM, 1977 (since reissued as *Tomorrow's Managers Today*).
5. Lifescript, or script, is now a well-known notion which is dealt with in some detail in the literature on transactional analysis–see, for example, Steiner, Claude, *Scripts People Live*, Bantam Books, 1975.

Checklist: Your own values

Use the following questions to review your own values and beliefs and see how well they fit with a transformational mentoring approach.

■ Which of the following beliefs do I hold?

- People are OK
- People want closeness
- People can change
- People want to grow
- We create our own meaning

    – We can make decisions
    – Our behaviour is purposeful

■ What other beliefs do I have that might be relevant within a developmental alliance?

■ What evidence do I have to support these beliefs?

■ What evidence do I have against these beliefs?

■ What impact might my beliefs have on the way I would function as a mentor?

■ What impact might my beliefs have on the way I would function as a mentee?

■ What impact might my beliefs have on the way I might introduce transformational mentoring into my organization?

■ What, if anything, do I need to do to confirm/check out/develop or otherwise update my beliefs?

6 How is a developmental alliance different?

Ownership and needs

At the risk of stating the obvious, the approach I am suggesting differs from the other mentoring approaches. The major distinction concerns ownership—in most other approaches the assumption is that the mentor knows best! What mentors know may be organizational politics, or specific technical expertise, or simply how to do the task. The aim is to transfer what they know, or can do, on to the mentee.

The developmental alliance, on the other hand, assumes that knowledge resides with the mentee. It may still be buried in their subconscious, but they do have it. Only they can know the full range of their wishes and concerns for the future—the function of mentors is to help mentees get in touch with their own preferences and make appropriate plans for their future development.

The other significant difference concerns whose needs are being met. Traditional mentoring (and all those other approaches that go under the same label) has a large element of 'organizational self-interest' involved. The mentor keeps in mind the needs of the organization as well as the interests of the mentee. In a developmental alliance, the requirements of the organization are not considered directly. They come in only as a factor affecting whether the mentee will be able to find suitable development opportunities doing work within the organization (i.e. should they stay there or do they need to go and work somewhere else?).

The three-cornered contract

Figure 6.1 shows three ways in which we can represent a three-cornered contract[1] between an organization, a mentor and a mentee. Version (a) represents a typical traditional mentoring arrangement; (b) is the equilateral triangle of a developmental alliance when operated within an organization; while (c) shows what may happen if the developmental alliance approach is misapplied.

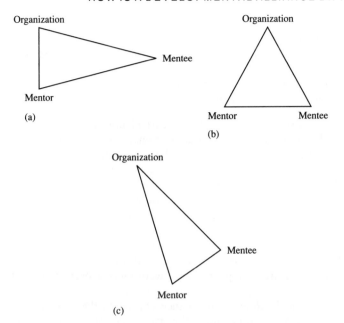

Figure 6.1   *Three-cornered contracts.*

Formal mentoring schemes

Diagram (*a*) illustrates the potential dilemma for many mentors in formal schemes. They are usually senior managers and hence have a 'duty' to the organization—to do their best to ensure that potential managers are being developed for the future. Often this results in the clones I referred to earlier. Even if not clones, the mentors in traditional schemes are still focused on providing a supply of suitable employees for promotion into management positions at some time.

Mentees 'collude' in this because they are employed by the organization. Whether they realize it or not, they implicitly accept the objective of the organization and the mentor. Indeed, they are often as committed to this as the mentor, believing that their future progress is inextricably linked to adopting the mentor as a role model.

Thus, the contract between the organization and the mentor consists of the mentor tacitly accepting the following 'messages' from the organization:

■ We employ you to be a senior manager.
■ We therefore expect you to work within the corporate norms.

■ We want you to use your best endeavours to develop more junior employees within those norms.
■ Your current evaluation will be influenced by how well you are seen to do this.
■ Your future employment will be affected by how well your mentees subsequently manage the organization.

In this 'contract', the mentee may well be regarded almost as an object, to be shaped and moulded to fit future organizational requirements.

This may sound somewhat cynical—until we recall that managers who operate outside organizational norms are not normally asked to be mentors. They may be tolerated, especially if they have some special skills that the organization needs, but they are not selected to pass on their perceived idiosyncrasies to more junior members of staff lest they 'contaminate' them.

There are a number of organizations in which attempts are currently being made to change the corporate culture. Many, however, are still selecting as mentors the very people who were most a part of the old guard, and new graduate entrants are being entrusted to these people. Were they to use a developmental alliance approach, they could have more junior people as mentors, and in this way could select those people who, in the past, had challenged the norms (and did not get promoted because they did not fit in). These 'renegades' would at least move away from the behavioural stereotypes that the organization wants to replace. It would even be possible for newly-employed graduates to mentor each other—again, this would at least avoid cloning the organization's dinosaurs.

The contract between the organization and the mentee in version (a) is along similar lines to that with the mentor:

■ We employ you to do a job.
■ We expect you to work within the corporate norms.
■ We want you to use your best endeavours to develop within those norms.
■ Your current evaluation will be influenced by how well you are seen to do this.
■ Your future employment will be affected by how well you are seen to do this.
■ We have allocated you a mentor who will help you to do this.

By implication, therefore, the mentor is well regarded within the organization. Any sensible new recruit will therefore see the mentor as a role model—the observed behaviour of whom will carry more weight than any written mission statement or other pronouncements about a changing corporate culture.

This will reinforce the messages that were probably picked up at the time of recruitment or promotion—you seem to be our type of person so we are selecting you as a high flyer worthy of mentoring support. A similar signal goes out to employees who do not have mentors. In this case, the implication is that, if you want to succeed here, you need to be more like these mentees and mentors. If you want to feel that the triangle has sides of equal length, you, too, must accept the constraints and responsibilities under which the mentor functions. If you want to minimize the *psychological distance* between you and the organization, then use your mentor as a role model.

The third side of the triangle—the contract between mentor and mentee—is heavily influenced by the explicit or implicit agreements with the organization. Often the contracting process is restricted to discussions about the *modus operandi*. The underlying assumptions about corporate culture may never be mentioned directly. It is simply accepted that the mentee is there to learn to copy the mentor—all they have to do is agree a suitable method for interacting with each other while they accomplish this.

Because the mentor is so often more senior, the issues of dependency and responsibility may also be taken for granted. The mentor is seen as the teacher and the mentee as the pupil. The mentee's job is to learn all that they can from the mentor, who in turn aims to pass on wisdom. The mentor 'knows' so the mentee 'receives'—and potential new approaches to tasks, to organizational and individual development and to independent decision making are lost in the process.

Developmental alliances within organizations

Diagram (*b*) illustrates the nature of a developmental alliance operated within an organization. The psychological distances between the parties are now equal—hence the equilateral triangle.

The contracts around employment between the organization and the mentor and the organization and the mentee are, of course, still there. However, some of the elements have changed significantly. Now, the organization is signalling to the mentor:

■ We employ you.
■ We trust you, and your colleagues, to work for the good of the organization.
■ You have our backing to help others to develop themselves, provided that the work is also being done.
■ We do not expect to attain organizational benefit by sacrificing individuals.

■ We want employees to develop themselves as much as possible, even if this ultimately means leaving this organization.

and to the mentee:

■ We employ you but recognize that we cannot realistically promise life-time employment.
■ We expect you to do the work for which we are paying you.
■ We encourage you to develop yourself.
■ We accept your right to decide that your long-term interests might be better served if you leave this organization.

With these two contracts, there is a balance between the organization and the individual. The organization is paying for the labour of the employee and therefore expects to receive a fair return. However, at the same time the organization recognizes that human beings will naturally grow and develop and want more challenges which may not be available within the organization.

Mentors are allowed to concentrate on helping mentees to decide where their future lies. They are not expected to encourage mentees to neglect the work they are being paid to do, but they are free to explore a range of options with the mentees. These might well relate to long-term growth outside the organization, as well as ways of preparing for that.

The contract between mentor and mentee is therefore much broader. There is no implicit expectation that the mentor should be a role model—why copy when the mentee may not be staying within the organization (a much more realistic assumption in today's employment market!). Instead, the mentor is there as a skilled questioner and listener, whose main aim is to help the mentee to clarify her or his own aspirations and work out how best to implement them.

Mentoring mutiny

Diagram (c) relates to what happens when mentors become too close to mentees—they encourage them to neglect the needs of the organization. This is not unlike incitement to mutiny—sometimes with similar results for the mutineers!

In this case, the contract between mentor and organization has disintegrated. The mentor has identified so much with the mentee that who pays the salary is forgotten. The psychological distance between mentor and organization is so great that the mentor might as well be operating independently.

The contract between mentee and organization may also become psychologically distant. Mentor and mentee then collude (perhaps unwittingly but sometimes deliberately) to ignore the requirements and rights of the organization and focus solely on the needs of the mentee.

Such a situation may happen when, for example, mentors believe they have been badly treated by the organization. Perhaps they feel that they have been passed over for promotion, or that their responsibilities have been reduced, or they perceive that their status has been eroded. They may then lose commitment to the organization and encourage mentees to 'take' whatever they can while they have the chance. This form of 'mentoring' may well occur in organizations which are announcing redundancies or restructurings.

The other impetus for such close mentor/mentee identification is the *Rescuer/Victim*[2] syndrome. With this dynamic, the mentor operates on the premise that they are there to save the mentee from the machinations of the organization—which is often seen as something remote being run by faceless senior managers. This style may also occur when the mentor believes that the mentee has an unreasonable manager. The 'rescuing' mentor therefore sets out to teach the mentee how to bend the rules for maximum personal advantage.

A third route to this closeness between mentor and mentee may occur when the mentor is not a senior manager—paradoxically, the format for a developmental alliance may give rise to a lack of commitment to the organization. This happens when such mentoring arrangements are taken for granted. If people are expected to act as mentors without being given training, without being allowed sufficient time and without it being clearly valued by the organization, they will treat mentoring as just another chore. They may then form alliances with mentees to pay lip service to the system.

The four-cornered contract

A more realistic, and more complex, way of looking at the nature of mentoring is shown in Figure 6.2. This takes into account the additional role of the manager of the mentee. We thus have 'contracts' between organization and mentor, organization and mentee, organization and manager; and between mentor and mentee, mentor and manager, and mentee and manager.

This is often the way in which mentoring currently operates within organizations. It raises several potential issues and sources of conflict, mainly between the mentor and the manager. The unlucky mentee may be caught in the middle.

The contract between the mentor and the mentee may be the same as I described under the three-cornered contract; in summary:

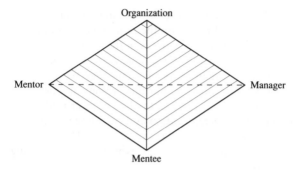

Figure 6.2 *The four-cornered contract.*

■ Be a manager
■ Work within the norms
■ Develop others to do the same.

The contract between the organization and the manager may be very similar, but there will be an additional emphasis:

■ Get the job done by your subordinates.

The contract between the mentee and the organization is unchanged.

The difficulties arise when the mentor believes that the future requirements of the organization are more important than the current needs as perceived by the manager. The mentor wants to initiate activities that will equip the mentee for a future role, while the manager wants the mentee to stay focused on the current tasks. Even managers who genuinely want to develop their staff sometimes have problems with this—the more so if they are under heavy pressure to maximize resources (as most are nowadays).

This will, of course, happen even with a developmental alliance. However, it is then clearly the responsibility of the mentee to decide how to balance commitment to the organization against the desire for self-development for the future. There is no conflict between mentor and manager here.

However, within many formal schemes the mentor is a more senior manager than the mentee's immediate manager. They may even be within the same 'chain of command' as the manager. This makes it difficult for the manager to protest about any suggestions that are seen to come from the mentor. Pointing out that developmental activities will clash with getting the job done may earn the manager a reputation for complaining. It is often less risky to do the work yourself to avoid being seen as undermining a senior manager.

A further issue which arises with the four-cornered contract is over the sharing of information. This is similar to the problem that can occur in the running of assessment centres. Mentors (and assessors) become privy to information relating to an individual's suitability for a future position. If this information is shared with the current manager, it is often misapplied to the present job. A mentee who needs further development before promotion may find that this information is being used out of context in the current evaluation.

Going outside the organization

I considered adding a further diagram, but it would have been simply a straight line. This is the developmental alliance option when it is operated with a mentor outside the organization (or by a mentee who is working independently).

In this case, there is only one contract—between mentor and mentee. The content of the contract does not have to include the requirements of an organization (although, again, the sensible mentee will take these into account when weighing up options).

Where a developmental alliance approach is in operation, anyone within an organization can make the decision that self-development matters. Individuals can therefore select their own mentors, who need not reflect the corporate values from the past. Such mentors might come from outside or inside the organization. This free choice of mentors would bring in fresh perspectives—and there can be few organizations nowadays that would not benefit from this.

Mentoring, coaching and counselling

I have concentrated so far on the differences between a developmental alliance and traditional mentoring. It is also worth contrasting a developmental alliance with coaching and counselling—especially since peer coaching is becoming increasingly common. In Figure 6.3, the overlapping circles show how these three approaches have some similarities and some differences[3]. Note that I am thinking here of counselling as it is generally provided at the workplace, and not of counsellors in private practice who may well be operating quite differently.

Mentoring, coaching and counselling all utilize some core skills, such as establishing rapport, listening, questioning, summarizing and giving feedback. They may use these skills somewhat differently, but the basic actions are similar and the skills are potentially transferable.

For instance, the focus of feedback will be different. In a coaching

Figure 6.3 *Mentoring, coaching and counselling.*

environment the feedback will be concentrated on the performance—is the person doing whatever the coach has recommended? Within a counselling relationship, the feedback is likely to be about the way in which the person is interacting. People often seek counselling for relationship problems, and the way they interact with the counsellor can provide clues about the impact they may be having on other people. This aspect may also be significant within a developmental alliance—but may well be extended into feedback about the overall process between mentor and mentee. This feedback may then include comments on the relationship between mentor and mentee, how they are functioning together, elements of the analysis of trends and how these may be affecting the developmental alliance itself, and so on.

The purpose of using a core skill may also vary, as shown for questioning. Questions are used during coaching to check learning. This may be learning that has occurred as a result of the coaching itself or it may be to establish a prior level of knowledge before the coaching begins. In counselling, however, questioning is used to raise the awareness of the counsellee. Unskilled counsellors sometimes fall into the trap of asking questions because *they* want to know the answers because they think that *they* are going to solve the problem for their client. Skilled counsellors know that this only leads to rejection or recriminations when their 'advice' does not work out as hoped. Questioning within a developmental alliance goes further than awareness because it is intended to stimulate learning.

This is a somewhat simplified picture—obviously there are overlaps in the ways in which questions are used. However, the major reason for asking them differs. So we might use questions to stimulate learning in a coaching session, but that will be a choice of teaching method. The main focus will still be on checking what the person has learned. Our main concern within counselling will be to cause the client to bring information into consciousness. Our questioning within an alliance will be more wide-ranging because we want mentees to understand their own functioning across a broad spectrum rather than related to a specific issue.

Different perspectives

If we now include traditional mentoring, we have four approaches to consider. Figure 6.4 shows a way of doing this, by contrasting the different perspectives between traditional mentoring, developmental alliances, coaching and counselling. The vertical axis has two dimensions: whether the approach is person-led or organization-led, and 'who knows best'. The horizontal axis varies from a short-term, specific focus to a long-term, broad focus.

A developmental alliance has a long-term, broad focus, is person-led (with the organization's needs being considered but coming a definite second), and is based on a belief that the mentee knows best. The mentor in an alliance is there to help the mentee identify opportunities for growth and development. To do this, mentors need far more than the rapport I mentioned earlier as a core skill—they need to create a bond.

Coaching is diametrically opposed to a developmental alliance on this model. Coaching is short-term, with a specific focus, such as a set of tasks about which the coach has expert knowledge. The coach aims to help the 'pupil' develop the skills that the organization requires. Coach and pupil need to establish rapport for this, but it will not be too serious if their relationship goes no deeper. This is particularly so as long as the pupil accepts that the skills are necessary—a keen student will learn in spite of a poor teacher.

Counselling in the workplace also tends to be a relatively short-term approach with a specific focal point. Rather than teaching a task, the counsellor sets out to help, or enable, the client to solve problems that the client has already identified. The requirements of the organization are usually suspended. More than rapport is needed for this; the good counsellor is empathic. Indeed, research confirms that the ability to empathize is far more important than any theoretical training the counsellor may have.

Figure 6.4   *Different perspectives.*

Finally, we have traditional mentoring. This has a long-term, broad focus. The mentor is assumed to know best, having the greater knowledge and experience. Mentors are also expected to take account of the needs of the organization. They are in the business of providing opportunities so that the mentee can develop into a more useful employee. They need to relate well to the mentee, who will use them as a role model of how to succeed within the culture of the organization.

Notes

1. Three-cornered contracts are based on an original idea by Fanita English, as developed by Nelly Micholt in 'Psychological Distance and Group Interventions', in *Transactional Analysis Journal*, Vol. 22, No. 4, October 1992, pages 228–33.
2. Rescuer and Victim are roles in the 'Drama Triangle'–see Karpman, Stephen, 'Fairy Tales and Script Drama Analysis' in *Transactional Analysis Bulletin*, 7(26), 1968, pages 39–43.
3. For more ideas about the differences between coaching and mentoring, plus

an additional contrast with instructing, there is a questionnaire designed by David Megginson which is reproduced in *The Learning Company* by Mike Pedler, John Burgoyne and Tom Boydell, McGraw-Hill, 1991. This book also contains useful ideas about organizational transformation.

Checklist: Who does what?

At this point you might like to refer back to the checklist in Chapter 1.

- Who are the mentors in your organization? How well do they fit the norms of the organization? What is the impact of this?
- Who are the mentees? How are they 'selected'? What is the impact of this?
- Draw the three- or four-cornered contracts that apply. How many corners (more than four)? How long are the lines? Are they balanced?
- How clearly differentiated are coaching, counselling and mentoring approaches in your organization?
- Do managers undertake coaching, counselling and/or mentoring? How clear are the boundaries?
- Using Figure 6.4 as a basis, what level of activity in each quadrant occurs within your organization?

7 The benefits (and drawbacks) of developmental alliances

With all those activities called mentoring that I described in Chapter 4, it may seem superfluous to add yet another. However, there are a number of advantages of a developmental alliance that traditional mentoring does not provide. Key among these are the way in which it opens up development processes to many more people; the impact it has on corporate cultures; and the way these two strands combine to produce a holistic approach to human growth—and hence ultimately to the productivity of organizations.

Availability

If I had to select only one way in which a developmental alliance improves on traditional mentoring, it would be that it makes the developmental process available to everyone who wants to be involved, whether as mentor, mentee or both.

Open to all

Anyone can have the advantages that were previously restricted to a selected few. There is no need to wait for the organization to start a mentoring scheme. There is no need to wait until it reduces the numbers at management levels. No-one has to stand by while others are selected as high fliers. They can seek out possible mentors at any time, even going outside the organization if necessary.

The approach may be even more valuable to the self-employed, since an alliance does not require that mentor and mentee work within the same organization (or within any organization). With so many organizations now using 'outsourcing', facilities management, management buyouts and so on, the numbers of people working outside large corporations is steadily increasing. These people are too valuable a part of the human resources of the country (world?) to be left without arrangements for their development.

Mentor availability

Using less senior people as mentors means that more people can volunteer. This eliminates the problems of potential mentee numbers exceeding available mentor numbers. We now have a larger pool of candidates from which to draw. In turn, mentors need have fewer mentees per head; each mentor can limit the hours served, so that even the very busy may now volunteer. An extra bonus is the fact that mentors with fewer mentee commitments will have more time to continue with their own developmental activities.

We can also look outside the organization for our mentors. I mentioned earlier that one association has done this for isolated professionals. As more people leave large organizations and set themselves up as small businesses, there will be a greater need for mentors who will operate across company boundaries. The pool of independents will be available as mentors to those still inside organizations, and vice versa. This approach will also fit the trend towards partnerships between suppliers and buyers. We can consolidate preferred supplier status by exchanging mentors.

Equal opportunities

The second most significant advantage is in the arena of anti-discriminatory practice. The traditional style of mentoring has a major inherent problem when we have cultural or gender differences (which is, of course, practically always). All too often, the only senior managers available as mentors are male and white. If we are to implement equal opportunities, we need more ways of teaming up to help each other.

Forming a developmental alliance raises fewer issues about lack of empathy and understanding across cultural or gender boundaries. This is because the focus is on the resources and the decisions of the mentee and on the facilitating skills, rather than on the previous experience of the mentor. This gives us options of matching or not matching mentor and mentee by race or gender; the final decision can be made by the mentee to suit personal circumstances at the time.

I am not suggesting that every mentee must have a mentor who exactly matches them in terms of race and gender. Mentors and mentees might choose to be similar or different. However, it is important that the *choice* is there. This can only occur to any extent if we draw our mentors from a much larger pool of potential than existing senior managers.

Organizational culture

Culture change

Introducing the concept of developmental alliances is in itself a useful marker of an intended change in the culture of an organization. Making it clear that all employees have the opportunity to have a mentor, that they are responsible for initiating this themselves, that they decide who the mentor will be, that they, too, can be mentors to others regardless of grade—all of these send powerful signals to the workforce about management's faith in their capabilities and potential.

Where an organization has already been 'delayered', the developmental alliance approach will reinforce the change. At the same time, it will provide a supportive environment for people who may be struggling to come to terms with suddenly changed perceptions of their own promotion prospects.

Community

Whether flatter or not, a similar process can be applied to organizations which intend to be true communities. We spend many hours a day working with other people; the quality of this time is an important contributor to our psychological and emotional health. The more our organization operates as a team, the happier and more productive we will be.

Again, we do not have to wait for the ideal state to be reached—we can use developmental alliances to initiate feelings of closeness and community. Whenever one person gives time and attention to listen and communicate with another, that person is creating a small island of community. Whenever people put aside their own assumptions and really listen to the other person, they are transcending individual differences. This level of attention, respect and caring is often associated only with counselling, but this restricts it to occasions when a problem exists. There is no reason why we should not extend this same spirit of community to help each other with the normal process of growth and development.

Changing the role models

It is difficult for mentors who have worked successfully within an organization for many years to change so completely that they can model a new corporate style to their mentees. Traditional mentoring schemes therefore tend to reinforce the status quo—even when management have decided that change is needed. The best intentioned human being will still say one thing and, out of awareness, do another.

Even when new senior managers are brought in, there is a problem if their role modelling is done via mentoring. The organizational cultures being developed nowadays usually incorporate a high degree of initiative and responsibility at all levels and in all jobs. This does not sit appropriately with a mentoring process that relies on mentees copying their mentors. If senior managers intend to be role models, they need to do so in ways which can be observed by all employees and copied only when the individual is satisfied that the model is a good one for them.

A key benefit here is avoidance of the dependency relationships so often associated with mentoring. Clarification that the relationship is intended to be between equals serves to remind mentees that they are still responsible for making their own decisions and choices. At the same time, the mentor is encouraged to recognize and deal with any inclinations towards 'rescuing' the mentee.

Customer care

There can be few organizations left untouched by the great customer care revolution. Giving better customer care needs staff who will show initiative and make decisions on the spot. This applies equally to 'customers' who are internal or are patients, rate-payers, clients or even prisoners. We are unlikely to develop relevant behaviours while organizations persist with the notion that only managers know what is appropriate—especially when it comes to something as important as a person's future career path. Taking charge of discussions about our own development is excellent practice for taking charge when we are the person dealing with a customer.

Learning organizations

An equally topical subject is the creation of learning organizations. These need employees to be engaged in a process of continuous development so that they can feed their own learning back into the organization. If we leave it to managers to stimulate this learning, they will have an impossible task. Individuals need to be actively involved in planning and initiating their own developmental activities. In this way, they help to create learning organizations and hence provide themselves with an environment where growth is seen as necessary and valued.

Quality

Similarly, the notion of total quality management (TQM) has become an important element of organizational life. True quality management involves everyone in the organization—with each person building quality into everything they do. This is another good reason for doing all we can to think and act for ourselves.

Potential

There are a number of options related to developing 'people potential'. We might train them on- or off-the-job, assess them and give feedback, involve them in continuous professional development, introduce S/NVQs, use temporary assignments, etc. In each of these, having a mentor can increase the learning.

Training

People can use an alliance to gain more from training courses, especially those aimed at their personal development. These programmes often include an element of mentoring in any case, when participants are invited to pair up to share experiences and ideas. Working with the developmental alliance stages will help them to get more from this process. After the programme ends, they will also be better able to initiate and maintain ongoing support networks with fellow participants.

These networks will not be restricted to people who attended the same course. There will usually be others who took the same programme on different dates. Wider networks can be created, and spot mentoring sought from a range of people depending on needs.

Competences

An additional option is to link a developmental alliance into any organizational initiatives about competences. Many organizations are introducing a focus on sets of competences, or characteristics, that are associated with success in the job. They tend, then, to provide ways for employees to be assessed against the criteria. This may be by using assessment or development centres, where participants engage in simulations of everyday tasks so that managers or colleagues can assess their performance. Most of these programmes include developmental feedback to participants, who are encouraged to devise and implement their own action plans.

Participants on such programmes can follow this up by identifying one or more people to mentor them afterward—perhaps one person for an ongoing mentoring relationship and others to cover specific areas, such as when they want to consider their own competences in terms of their likely prospects in a particular department. Even those not attending assessment programmes could use a mentor to help them draw up a plan for obtaining feedback from others.

Where these initiatives are linked to continuous professional development, S/NVQs or other approaches requiring production of a portfolio, a mentor can act as a neutral sounding board. Rather than functioning as an assessor, whose job is really to check that the evidence is available, an independent mentor can help the mentee to make sure that genuine self-development is happening and not simply the collection of documentation for a logbook. In this way, the energy that once might have been used to focus on manipulating the organizational system, or to get good ratings at appraisal time, can now be applied fully to the development activity.

Peter principle

Being more confident about our own opinions regarding development will help us to avoid the *Peter Principle*[1]. This well-known concept refers to the habit that organizations have of developing a form of blindness to any development other than via promotion. When this happens, people are promoted until they reach their own level of incompetence. In this way, organizations manage to lose their best craftspeople by making them into poor supervisors, and their best technicians by expecting them to manage people. They take competent, confident employees and turn them into anxious, incompetent senior employees who have been promoted beyond their capabilities.

Setting up a developmental alliance, where the focus of the mentor is clearly on helping the mentee rather than taking care of organizational needs, will avoid this pitfall. A personal mentoring process which is not linked to promotion will help mentees to sidestep the pressures. They can decide how best to maintain their ongoing development at a level that suits their abilities and preferences.

The drawbacks

It would be foolish to pretend that there are no drawbacks associated with the introduction of developmental alliances. Most of them are shared with traditional mentoring, but may be perceived as more severe when associated with a developmental alliance. These disadvantages relate to the shortage of suitable mentors, to the time involved, to perceived conflict with the roles of personnel and line managers, to the difficulties of monitoring and controlling the quality of mentoring provided, and to the danger of demotivation when people realize that their potential exceeds their opportunities.

Suitable mentors

Although a developmental alliance approach means that mentors can be found at any level of an organization's hierarchy, or even outside it, there is still a danger that people will volunteer for the wrong reasons. In

Chapter 9 I describe the range of characteristics that an effective mentor needs; self-awareness is an important consideration.

People often have unconscious motives. For example, they may volunteer to be a mentor because they want to please senior management, because they think it will look good on their CV, or because they want to be a counsellor but can't find a counselling organization that will take them on. Once a mentor, they may not realize that they are pushing their own opinions onto the mentee, or that they are living a new career vicariously through the mentee, or that they have sided with the mentee in opposition to the organization.

Conversely, there may be a shortage of suitable volunteers because the concept is new, because people lack self-confidence in their ability to be of help to others, because of fears of seeming to get 'above their station' in the eyes of managers and colleagues.

Time

Any developmental activity takes time. This has always been an issue with traditional mentoring schemes, and will probably continue to be an area of difficulty. Successful people tend to be picked as mentors and successful people tend to have many demands on their time. More time is spent on travelling when mentor and mentee are in different locations.

Managers have also been known to complain that their staff should be hard at work instead of spending (wasting) time being mentored. (They say the same about some training courses.) There is a risk that they will react even more negatively if their staff member is being mentored by a more junior rather than a more senior person.

The issue about the time taken is, of course, an artificial drawback. If we do not spend time developing people, our organizations will cease to exist after a while because we are not growing new ideas, new skills, new abilities to match the need for change in the world. And there is no evidence to prove that seniority is a prerequisite for helping someone else to arrive at sensible conclusions about their own future.

Conflict

Again, this is something of an artificial drawback. The conflict is mainly perceptual. Mentor, manager, personnel professional—each believe that they should have sole responsibility for the development process. They may also be convinced that only they have the relevant skills.

Instances of real conflict also occur. When a mentor is also a senior manager, there is more risk that the temptation will arise to arrange 'opportunities' for the mentee which impinge on the plans of the mentee's manager. Similarly, personnel professionals may focus more on developmental options than on the manager's need to get the job done.

In some ways, these difficulties may be *reduced* with a developmental alliance. This is because the mentor is no longer senior to the mentee and will therefore not have the organizational authority to arrange things for the mentee. Instead, the mentor has to leave it to the mentee to make the decision—while challenging the mentee to consider all aspects of the situation, including the manager's expectations. The mentor cannot 'lean' on the manager by virtue of that manager's organizational position.

Mentoring quality

Another common area of concern about mentoring is how to monitor and control the quality of what gets done. It is intrusive (and time consuming) to observe mentoring sessions. Asking mentees to evaluate their mentors may not get at the truth if the mentors are able to influence the future prospects of the mentees—sensible mentees will hesitate over complaining about people who may be on the panel for their next promotion interview. Such evaluations may also be unfair to mentors who have unwilling or incompetent mentees.

Other options for assessing the quality of mentoring include checking out during mentor training programmes and doing a quantitative check by analysing how regularly mentor and mentee meet. Neither method is very reliable, however. Performance during training may be much easier to sustain (with an obliging role player) or much harder to achieve (in such an artificial situation). Counting the meetings takes no account of the quality of the interactions.

As with conflict, this is an area where a developmental alliance may make it easier to gauge the quality of the mentoring. If we are choosing our own mentors, and they are not senior to us, then we will be unlikely to continue the relationship if it fails to be helpful to us. Mentees will vote with their feet!

The lack of direct information will still be perceived as a problem by some people. They may lack confidence in the ability of a mentee to make an informed decision about whether the sessions are useful. This might well be the case for a 'naive' mentee who has no prior experience of mentoring. It may be necessary to take the success of the mentoring on trust.

Demotivation

This drawback is one shared by all approaches which help people to recognize their own capabilities. Assessment and development centres, for example, have been known to lead to loss of key employees. This is because they have applied for jobs elsewhere after receiving feedback that gave them a much higher opinion of their own strengths than they had held previously.

This is a difficult drawback to rebut—providing mentoring more widely may indeed lead people to recognize that their potential is higher than the opportunities for growth available within their current organization. If they do not leave, there is a strong possibility that they will feel demotivated at the lack of prospects. It will not necessarily be linked to their promotion chances, but may simply be boredom if they are not able to continue learning and adding to their skills.

I mentioned earlier in this chapter how a developmental alliance approach can form part of a culture change initiative. Back in Chapter 5 I listed the values and beliefs which I think are essential if this new form of mentoring is to succeed. These two aspects—culture and values—are the real answers to the problem of demotivation. Organizations will, in the future, need to become places where people are growing all the time and where this growth is an important element within the value system of the organization. When this happens, it will be seen as natural for people to seek employment elsewhere if their development needs cannot be matched to the needs of their current employer. It will also be more likely that their current organization is changing and adapting fast enough for there to be plenty of opportunities for growth within it.

Notes

1. Peter, Laurence J. and Hull, Raymond, *The Peter Principle: Why Things Always Go Wrong*, Souvenir Press, reissued 1992.

Checklist: The pros and cons

Use the following list to consider the pros and cons of introducing developmental alliances (or some other form of mentoring) into your organization.

For each item (and any others you want to add), describe briefly the situation that applies or is likely to apply.

Then, allocate a score out of 10 (or 100 if you want finer distinctions) in the appropriate column to reflect how much of a positive or negative factor each item is.

Finally, add up the scores as if this were a balance sheet. Check whether you have enough positives 'in the bank' to support taking action at this time.

If the result is not positive enough, decide whether it is feasible for you to work out what needs to change and draw up a plan of action.

Item	Brief description	Positive score	Negative score
open to all			
mentor availability			
equal opportunities			
culture change			
community			
changing role models			
customer care			
learning organization			
quality			
training			
development			
competences			
Peter principle			
time			
conflict			
mentoring quality			
demotivation			
Total			

8 The stages of a developmental alliance

So far I have only given a fairly brief outline of the various stages of a developmental alliance. Before going on to suggest how the approach might be introduced within an organization, let me now spell out in more detail what is involved. I will describe the main elements of each stage, together with some suggestions about the skills, knowledge, attitudes and so on that will be needed.

I have had to make some choices about the level of detail in this chapter. It is not intended to be the definitive guide to transformational mentoring (or to any other style of mentoring)—that will be the next book! What I have aimed to do is describe the stages, show how various concepts from other settings may be applied and hopefully stimulate you to use your own ideas. I have assumed that you will be familiar with some of the material already, but have given references in case you want more background.

Alliance

The first stage is, of course, creating the alliance. There are three aspects to this: preparation, forming a bond and agreeing a contract. The better each phase is handled, the more powerful will be the alliance. These phases are part of the first stage of a process which may be going to last for up to two years, so care in the beginning is clearly justified.

Preparation

Preparation consists of what mentor and mentee do before they meet. This follows the actual choice of each other, which is something I will cover in more detail in later chapters. It is a good idea to work with a checklist prepared in advance. Such a list may be used by mentor and mentee; if each of them consider their responses beforehand, they can use the checklist as an 'agenda' of areas to discuss when they meet. After going through the lists, a combined version can be drawn up and used as a basis for later evaluation of the mentoring process.

It will be important to do this as a *joint* effort—the checklist belongs to both parties. A new mentee (or a new mentor) might be prompted by seeing a copy of their potential partner's list, but should still concentrate on drawing up their own set of priorities.

Examples of the content of such a checklist include:

- Why have I become a mentor/mentee?
- What do I offer/what do I want?
- What significant issues might arise?
- What do I feel strongly about?
- Which are the areas where I prefer my mentor/mentee to 'match' me; over which am I neutral; on which would I like us to be different?
- What about issues of trust and respect?
- What are my own psychological/personal/thinking/working styles?
- How do they affect the way I interact with others?
- What mentoring skills do I have/want my mentor to have?
- How much time will we have?
- Where will we meet?
- What mutual contacts are we likely to have? How might that affect the mentoring?
- What is my attitude towards self-development?
- Who is/has been a mentor to me? What did I gain?
- Who else is involved in this process (e.g. senior management, personnel, mentee's manager)?

Bonding

Once mentor and mentee start to work together, their first priority is to create a bond. The quality of this bond will have a major impact on the relationship that follows. The mentoring process often involves a mentee admitting to weaknesses; this is not something most of us feel comfortable doing except with someone we trust and respect. As we develop, we will also have successes to celebrate; we will want to feel that our mentor is close enough to us to share our delight. There may also be times when it is impossible to separate our work from our home lives; again, we will want to confide in our mentor if we are to have their help in thinking through our options.

An early element of bonding will be the establishment of rapport. Techniques from NLP[1] are now probably the simplest and best-known. Briefly, the premise here is that if we behave as if rapport has already been established, we will attain it much more quickly. When rapport is established (for example, between two friends in a social setting), we can observe they they match each other in four ways: through voice tone and tempo; via body posture; with their pattern of breathing; and through any repetitive movements or gestures. Sounds weird, but it really does work!

Clearly, establishing rapport is only one aspect of forming a relationship. A lot more will be needed as well. While we are busily matching these outward indicators, we also need to engage in conversation. Whether they have been considered in advance or not, sharing the responses to the checklists is a gentle way of continuing the bonding process. Particularly useful will be discussion of the aims—why the mentor has agreed to mentor, what the mentee hopes to achieve with the mentor's help. Getting to know each other by comparing styles will also get the process moving.

Another option is to work through the following aspects of the mentoring relationship together:

- *Compatibility*: What opinions do we share? What do we have in common?
- *Control*: Who will control what? How much does each of us like to control? How will we share control—mentee over content, mentor over process, perhaps?
- *Caring*: Do we have the ability to behave in a nurturing way towards each other? It is often assumed that only the mentor should be caring, but this creates a very one-sided, dependency-based relationship.
- *Closeness*: Real closeness occurs when both of us are able to be spontaneous—how will we show our emotions and let each other know how we really feel? Genuine emotions include anger, sadness and fear as well as happiness.
- *Competence*: Two heads are better than one—working together in a logical mode will increase our mutual abilities to problem solve and get decisions made. How best can we do this?
- *Cooperation*: How will we do this? What are our previous experiences of cooperation like? How flexible can we be?
- *Challenge*: Two heads should be better than one—how will we challenge each other?

And for the potential drawbacks:

- *Conformity*: Are we in any danger of conforming for the sake of it?
- *Conflict*: How will we handle conflicts and avoid spending valuable time in arguments?

And finally:

- *Contracting*: How can we use the contracting process to reinforce our genuine connection with each other?

Contracting

Contracting is needed in two formats—as an agreement about the longer-term developmental alliance, and as a specific arrangement for a specific mentoring session. Contracting ensures that we are clear about what is likely to happen, what our respective roles and responsibilities are, how we expect each other to behave. Although the term has a legal meaning, it is now commonly used for verbal agreements between people. These agreements are never going to be discussed in a court of law, but they do add considerably to the quality of the interactions.

There are several significant benefits from having a contract:

- Both parties have a clear idea of the purpose of the interactions.
- It clarifies respective roles as mentor and mentee.
- It ensures that the right person—the mentee—determines the purpose and direction of the mentoring.
- It makes explicit the responsibilities as mentor and mentee.
- It gives the opportunity to agree methods of working together.
- It sidesteps potential problems of either party changing the ground rules in the future without mutual agreement by making it clear that this would be a breach of the contract.
- It provides a mechanism by which either party can seek agreement to a change.
- It reassures both that the other person is taking the arrangement seriously.
- It helps to start and build the mentoring relationship.
- It encourages healthy bonding, with both parties learning that they need to be honest about what they will and will not do within the relationship.
- It reinforces the fact that they have mutual responsibilities for the mentoring process.
- It takes care of the administrative aspects, such as arrangements to meet regularly.
- It establishes boundaries, so that both parties know where mentoring stops and how it might fit in with other contact that they have with each other.
- It makes them think about what they are going to be doing!

Contracting can be thought of in four layers.

The *procedural contract* encompasses the administrative aspects, such as when, where and how often to meet, length of sessions, length of mentoring relationship itself (single session, several weeks, months, years).

The *professional contract* clarifies the roles and responsibilities of mentor and mentee. This includes aspects such as the purpose of the mentoring; what does the mentee want to achieve; what skills, abilities, advice, expertise does the mentor bring to the process; the boundaries to the mentoring; what topics will/will not be discussed; what about confidentiality?

The *personal contract* level focuses on how mentor and mentee will interact: what styles of interacting do they have; how will they support and challenge each other; how will conflict be handled; how will success be celebrated; what are each party's learning goals?

The *psychological contract* consists of the undercurrents which are often outside our awareness—at least until we force ourselves to consider them. This level is the most potent; problems here will sabotage the process in ways that are hard to detect. Although these manoeuvres can often be observed by third parties, this option is not available within the mentoring relationship. Mentor and mentee therefore need to take special care with this level. Questions they might ask themselves include: In what ways have we unwittingly sabotaged relationships in the past; if this process were going to fail, how might that happen; how will we share process concerns with each other?

The suggestions above relate to a long-term contract, which might typically be planned to last for about 18 months. In that case, review periods should be built in—perhaps after about four sessions and then after each six-month period. Unless there is an instant antipathy, it is not usually a good idea to review the contract too quickly. Fewer than four sessions does not really give the partners a proper chance to experience working together; they are likely to apply too much attention to evaluating the process rather than getting down to business. This is why counsellors ask clients to commit to a minimum number of sessions; otherwise they are reluctant to challenge in case the client 'runs away'.

An abbreviated version of the contracting process is needed for each session. This might consist of:

Procedural
How long have we got today?

Professional
What specific aspect are we going to work on?
Is this new or a continuation of previous work?
What does the mentee want to have achieved by the end of the session?
Does that seem feasible to the mentor?
How shall we work together this time?

Personal
What successes shall we celebrate?
What setbacks do we need to deal with?

Psychological
How open and effective is the process between us?
Do we need to deal with any issues?

The contract with the organization

In Chapter 6 I described the three- and four-cornered contracts that often apply when mentoring is conducted within an organization. The ideas on contracting listed above will need to be extended when there are other parties involved.

For the procedural level, what limitations does the organization impose on times and locations of meetings; are there any expectations about keeping records? For the professional aspect, what view of mentoring exists in the organization; what is the formal relationship between the mentor and the mentee's manager; what are the contracts between the mentor, the mentee, the manager and the organization; what training or other support will the organization provide to the mentor and to the mentee? How might the personal level be affected by the organizational context? And at the psychological level, how healthy is the organizational culture; what games get played in the organization; how does the mentee's manager really feel about the mentoring arrangement?

Note: contracts are not meant to be cast in stone! Legal contracts might require a court to alter them, but there are still usually provisions somewhere within the law for such change. When we make mentoring contracts, we need to recognize that human beings make a habit of growing and changing—indeed, that is the aim of mentoring. Any contracts should therefore include specific references to ways for updating, amending and closing them.

Assessment

The second stage of the developmental alliance is rather like the first stage in many counselling models—it amounts to 'helping them tell their story'. The aim is to enable mentees to review their situation, to describe (for themselves) their current circumstances, how they got there and where they might consider going in the future.

The emphasis at this stage is on *description*; analysis and planning will come later. First, mentees need to clarify and identify their strengths and weaknesses, experiences, knowledge and skills, personal and professional circumstances. It is almost like producing an autobiography or performing a stock-take.

In a developmental alliance this stage is far more significant than it might be within traditional mentoring. In the latter, assessment of mentees is often undertaken by the organization, in the person of the manager, via an assessment centre or appraisal process, or even by the mentors. For transformational mentoring, it is imperative that mentees take the initiative and have full responsibility for their own assessment.

This is why the mentors will need to show genuine interest, and skill, in getting the mentees to talk. The core skills of listening and questioning will be essential. Some reflecting will also be appropriate, in order for the mentors to help the mentees keep track of the content. In addition, there are other aspects which may well occur at all stages but are particularly relevant during the assessment process: empathy and self-disclosure; mind-mapping and reality checking; and the initiation of a portfolio.

Empathy and self-disclosure

The rapport that was established during the first stage now needs to deepen into empathy. It is generally accepted that the effectiveness of a counsellor depends on that counsellor's ability to empathize rather than on any particular skills or counselling methods. Carl Rogers[2] wrote of client-centred therapy involving an attitude which sees the self-worth of everyone, respects rights to self-direction and is based on 'deep respect'. This cannot easily be learned since it arises from having caring and respectful beliefs and values about the innate worth of human beings.

True empathy involves the mentor sharing personal feelings and responses with the mentee. Such self-disclosure is an important part of helping the mentee to feel comfortable enough to likewise admit to weaknesses and talk about any concerns with the mentor. Any self-disclosure must be relevant to the needs of the mentee—the mentor can monitor this by checking that they have a clear idea of how the disclosure is intended to help the mentee.

Describing similar fears about career prospects, about working with difficult people, about making mistakes, may be helpful provided the conversation does not degenerate into a mutual moans session. So might describing the ways in which such worries were put into proper perspective. Telling the mentee about the mentor's current interpersonal difficulties, or gossiping about mutual acquaintances, would be an abuse of the mentoring relationship.

Deborah Tannen[3] writes of interesting gender differences affecting self-disclosure. She says that women typically self-disclose to share how they, too, have had a problem just like the one being described and that they know just how it feels. Men, on the other hand, tend to encourage in a very different way—they emphasize how easily the other person will be able to deal with the problem, and stress that it is really not such a big problem anyway. Both approaches are intended to be reassuring.

These are stereotypes, but are based closely enough on typical patterns to ring true. There will, of course, be some men who use the female style and some women who use the male style. Whichever style we opt for, it is important to note that we may have to practise so that we can select the one that the mentee would find most comfortable. Self-disclosure in the wrong mode will leave the mentee feeling even worse!

Mind-mapping and personal constructs

Mind-mapping and personal constructs are both models which are helpful at the assessment stage. A combination of the ideas of Tony Buzan[4] and George Kelly[5] provides a framework for understanding the process. It is as if the mentee is being invited to perform a 'brain dump'— to put out the contents of their mind for inspection.

Buzan suggests that the brain stores information in patterns, with major nodes and branches. Figure 8.1 shows an example, based on ideas generated at a meeting to discuss the developmental alliance approach. This would be just one pattern among many in a person's head. The range of patterns would in turn be linked via higher-order patterns. Putting the patterns down on paper produces a map of the mind.

This map shows only the topics. Figure 8.2 shows what happens if we repeat the process to produce two imaginary maps that might be held by a mentor about a mentee. We now see more clearly how different constructs lead us to different conclusions. Kelly's notion of personal construct theory tells us that many of the places on the map will have an either/or nature to them. This either/or, or *bi-polar dimension*, refers to our beliefs and opinions. For example, when talking about previous colleagues we may well have constructs such as: they were nice or nasty; friendly or taciturn; gracious or mean-minded; efficient or happy-go-lucky.

There is likely to be an overarching construct, such as whether we liked the person or not. Depending on our own self-image, liking may go with the other person being efficient, or it may attach to the person who is happy-go-lucky. Because of the clustering effect, we may also assume that all efficient people are taciturn and mean-minded—or that they are friendly and gracious.

Each of us has our own set of constructs, but some of these will overlap with the constructs of other people. This will happen more if we work together in the same organizational culture. In that case, we will develop some common dimensions on which to base our judgements about people, organizations and even life in general.

When we access our mind maps, we activate the corresponding constructs. Mentees describing part of their mind maps will therefore have much richer pictures than may be apparent from their first comments. Often this richness is overlooked by the mentors, whose own mind maps have been stimulated by the discussions. The mentors call up

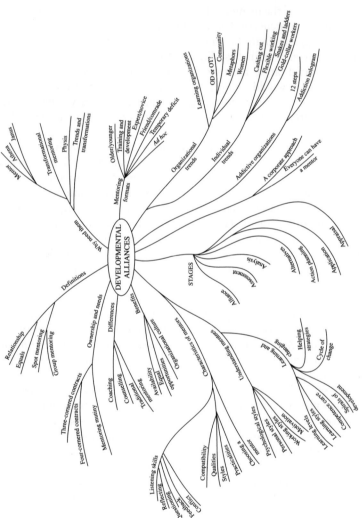

Figure 8.1   *A mind map of developmental alliances.*

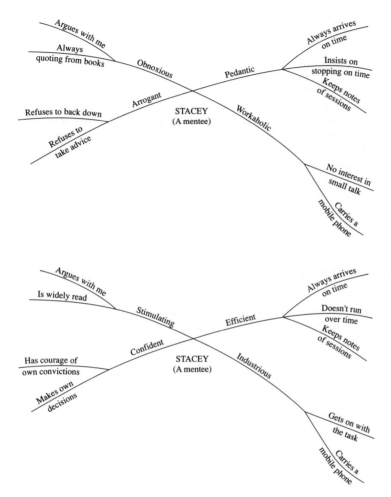

Figure 8.2 *Two imaginary mind maps.*

their own version, complete with their own constructs, and may never realize that they have different patterns to those held by the mentees.

For instance, imagine a mentee who is talking about a 'difficult boss'. The mentee's constructs around this may include a manager who insisted on very short timescales, which clashed with the construct that good performance was something that had been checked very carefully. The mentor, however, has a different view of a difficult boss. For them, the main construct associated with this concerns managers who shout at people. The mentor may tell the mentee 'I know just what you mean'. Mentor and mentee may believe they are talking about the same thing, but their maps are significantly different. The core skill of paraphrasing will help prevent such misinterpretations.

Portfolio building

During the assessment stage mentees will be generating a lot of information about themselves, as well as considering it in a way they may not have done before. It will probably be helpful if they start some kind of portfolio. This might be a fairly extensive project that would later serve as evidence if they wish to attain an S/NVQ or similar qualification. Alternatively, it might be a record for the purpose of certifying continuous professional development, as is being increasingly required by many professional bodies. Or it might simply be a development log or study journal—these can lead to a significant increase in the amount of learning that individuals can draw out from their experiences.

For an S/NVQ the mentee will probably need to consult a suitably qualified adviser and/or assessor before deciding on the content of the portfolio. However, there are some basic aspects that any mentor can suggest for inclusion:

- What have you achieved? To what standard or level?
- What evidence do you have of achievement? e.g. written, recorded using audio or video tape, computer-based (on disks or hard copy), photographs, models.
- Whose evidence? e.g. your own work, correspondence and commendations from customers, colleagues, managers.
- What have you learned during the development process? How have you learned it?
- What are you satisfied with? What do you still want to develop further?

As with the mentoring process itself, these questions can be related to an overall process or to a specific activity. Thus, the portfolio might reflect development spread over months or years, or it might be a learning diary which the mentee updates each week. The benefit to the mentoring process will come from the reviewing, and hence consolidating, of the learning.

Analysis

Once the mentee has 'told the story' and the mentor has helped them unpack their mind map, it is time to analyse—to look for themes and trends so that the mentee will better understand the meanings within the map. It will be important for the mentee to understand any form of analysis used—this will minimize the risk of the mentor becoming a surrogate analyst.

The core skills of listening and questioning, although still in use, become less significant during this stage. Reflecting skills take on more importance, particularly summarizing in ways which help to highlight patterns in the information. Feedback skills may also be needed, as the mentor prompts the mentee to consider their own part in previous events.

Lifelines

A simple yet powerful way of moving from the assessment to the analysis stage is to have the mentee draw a personal lifeline. A lifeline is a pictorial representation of significant events. It uses a horizontal scale of time and a vertical scale of 'feeling good', or success, or satisfaction or whatever else the mentee chooses. A line is drawn against these, starting at birth, to show the ups and downs of life. Notes about the sections of the line are added onto it, as shown in Figure 8.3

Drawing the lifeline and adding the notes helps mentees to understand their own history. They are able to see if there are any repeating patterns. Mentees can also look for similarities, such as how they felt each time they changed jobs. The increased awareness of their own reactions and behaviours will help them when they come to the stage of generating alternatives for the future.

This can be a very profound experience, since most people do not consider their whole life plan in this way. Doing it successfully will

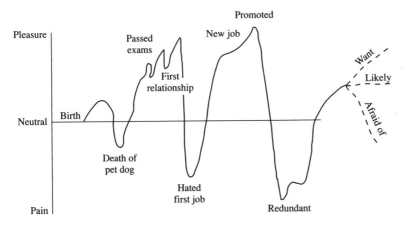

Figure 8.3 *An example of a lifeline.*

depend on the level of rapport and empathy established during the earlier stages of the mentoring relationship. As with all the techniques suggested in this book, it will help if the mentor has also completed the activity. Mentors will then be alert for possible sensitive areas and will be better able to self-disclose appropriately.

The lifeline can also be drawn speculatively into the future. Mentees can project:

- what they want to happen
- what they believe is likely to happen
- what they are afraid might happen.

Genograms

Another way of understanding our situation better is to sketch out a *genogram*[6]. This is a sort of mixture of a genealogical chart and an organization chart. Instead of levels of management, it shows our relatives back through the last few generations, as shown in Figure 8.4. Squares represent males, circles are females.

We are all influenced in varying degrees by our family backgrounds, as well as by our peers, the neighbours, the distant relatives who were nevertheless often quoted, our siblings, possibly even our pets. Even those who are brought up outside a family will have been affected by whatever took its place, such as a children's home or foster parents. Teachers, other staff and pupils at boarding schools will also play a part.

The genogram provides a visual way of identifying and understanding some of these influences. After sketching out the chart, notes are added about significant characteristics of individuals or particular ways in which the mentee has been influenced by them.

Questions for eliciting a genogram include:

- How many generations back are talked about in your family?
- Which family members do you know of in each generation?
- What do you know, or remember, about each of them:
  - How did they get on with each other?
  - How did they get on with people outside the family?
  - What positive qualities did they have?
  - What negative qualities did they have?
  - What contact did you have with them?
  - What impact did they have on you?
  - What do you know about their values and beliefs?
  - What do you know about how they behaved?
  - What was their quality of life like?
  - What was the balance for them between work, home, friends, etc?
- How have you been influenced by your predecessors?

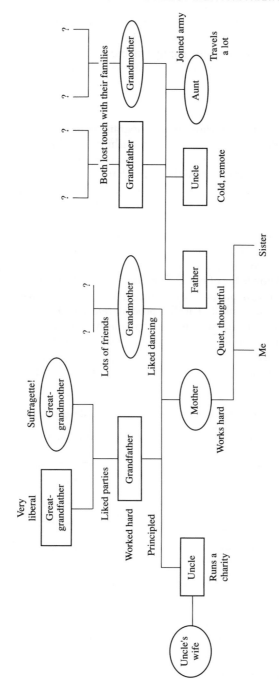

Figure 8.4   *An example genogram.*

■ What qualities do you share with any of them?
■ What mottoes or maxims of theirs do you now repeat?
■ How does your life parallel theirs?
■ How has your professional life been shaped by them?

Relationships

Completing a lifeline or a genogram is likely to stimulate mentees to consider the impact of relationships on their progress. There are numerous models available for understanding human behaviour, so I will not go into much detail here. In Chapters 9 and 10 I apply some of these frameworks to the psychological, personal and working styles of mentors and mentees. These same models could be used within the mentoring process, as could many others. It will be important that mentees become as knowledgeable as mentors about whichever models are used, so that the two work together at analysing. The mentor should not take on the 'expert' role in this.

A knowledge of *parallel process* will also be helpful, so that mentor and mentee can monitor for a repeat of any trends within the mentoring relationship itself. Parallel process refers to the way in which human interactions are so often unconsciously duplicated at different levels of contact. For instance, a person who is complaining about a difficult relationship with someone they supervise is likely to replay the same dynamic with the person who supervises them. This is shown in Figure 8.5.

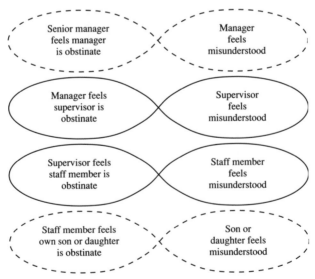

Figure 8.5 *A parallel process.*

Pat, the supervisor, complains that Chris is obstinate and does not accept the objectives set by Pat. Vijay, the manager, feels that Pat is obstinate and will not accept the objectives set by Vijay. This sounds weird, but it is surprising how often such a parallel process occurs. The dynamics are *out of awareness*, so Vijay and Pat do not usually recognize what is happening—they just feel very frustrated.

During the analysis stage this notion of parallel process can be particularly useful. If the mentor monitors personal reactions to the mentee, that mentor can often guess what might be happening in the mentee's relationship with someone else. A tentative and sensitive sharing of this will usually enable the mentee to identify the unhelpful dynamic. Once the process has been brought into awareness, it is relatively easy for the mentee to plan appropriate changes.

Strengths, weaknesses, opportunities and threats (SWOT)

Techniques for reviewing, such as a SWOT analysis, can be used to look at relationships, but can also be applied to cover a much wider perspective. Often used to assess the position of a company within the market, it can just as easily be applied to an individual.

Strengths may include skills, knowledge, experience, qualifications, and personal attributes such as enthusiasm—and should extend to qualities not currently being used. Weaknesses encompass a lack of any of the strengths; these may more easily be identified by using an appropriate list of criteria such as those produced for S/NVQs in areas of potential interest to the mentee. There is a general list of qualities needed for success in the corporate world of the nineties in Chapter 14.

Opportunities concern the environment surrounding the mentee. They may be related to freedom of movement between jobs, companies or locations and access to training and development, the chance to travel, and the availability of role models. Promotion prospects may seem an obvious area to include, although it may be more sensible to consider sideways moves in the flatter organizations which we now have. Other opportunities might be options for sabbaticals, family support, funding through grants, etc.

Threats also occur within the environment. These include the possibility (or likelihood) of redundancy, the impact of new technology or changes in working methods, the danger of falling behind as professional standards are raised and any possibility that prior conflicts may return or earlier problems re-emerge. As with the lifeline, the trends identified in Chapters 2 and 3 may be relevant when a mentee is preparing lists of opportunities and threats.

In addition to listing items under these four headings, weightings can be assigned. This will turn the analysis into a sort of human audit sheet.

It will then be possible, cautiously, to check the balance of assets against liabilities.

Alternatives

Having told the story, and analysed it, we move on to what is generally the second stage of a counselling approach—seeing things differently. Some new insights may well have emerged already. The aim now is to help the mentee to identify potential changes they might make, possible goals they might adopt and a wider range of options that are available to them. The mentor's core skills will still be important, but the focus of the questions will shift into stimulating thinking by the mentee. It becomes increasingly important for the mentor to use an appropriate helping strategy, as this is the stage where there is the most temptation to tell the mentee what to do.

Spot mentoring may avoid this, and will also minimize the risk of the primary mentor taking too much responsibility for action. Other mentors who have specialist experience may enable the mentee to identify a broader range of alternatives. Because spot mentoring is organized in single sessions, the mentee can arrange such meetings to cover a variety of settings. The role of the main mentor then becomes one of helping the mentee to collate the information obtained from spot mentors, so that more options are actively considered.

People often unwittingly overlook options because they have become accustomed to thinking in predetermined ways. Many of us lose the habit of being creative as we grow up. There are a number of reasons for this: perhaps we were ridiculed for our ideas, maybe we implemented an idea which led to negative consequences, or possibly we were told when we were small that we were just 'not very good at that sort of thing'. Whatever the reason, most adults lack the ability to be innovative that we all had as children. We therefore limit ourselves to the familiar and overlook significant opportunities for growth. A structured approach to problem solving and decision making can enable us to resurrect the awareness, creativity and commitment that we had when we were small.

Steps to success

I have related the following 'Steps to Success' framework to mentoring, so that it repeats the overall mentoring stages but with a specific focus. Thus, it goes from the assessment stage, through analysis and alternatives, and into action. By checking each stage for completion, we can ensure that areas are not being missed. This model can also be useful for spotting why an idea is not being applied—often we have a solution in search of a problem because the situation has not been correctly analysed.

- *Situation*: This is the assessment stage. It involves making sure that the mentee has correct and complete information about the situation. What is actually going on, what data do they have access to, what has happened in the past that now affects the present, and so on?
- *Significance*: This is the analysis stage. What is the significance of the information they have about the situation? What are the trends, what should they be preparing for, what are the problems or potential problems? How important are various aspects of the situation, what priorities are there?
- *Solutions*: This and the next step relate to the Alternatives stage of mentoring. What options are available? How can we generate more— brainstorming, spot mentoring, visits to other organizations, reading? We need to continue generating options until we are sure that we can identify no more. No solution should be rejected until we have measured it against the following steps.
- *Skills*: Having identified a range of options, we need to consider how skilfully the mentee might implement them. Many people drop good ideas at this point because of an incorrect belief that they lack the necessary ability. The SWOT analysis described earlier in this chapter should have generated a longer list than normal of the mentee's skills. Alternatively, a check against an S/NVQ criteria list should stimulate ideas.

  Even lack of a skill should not automatically eliminate an idea from the list of options. Acquiring new skills may become part of the subsequent action plan. Mentees may need to be reminded that they probably have additional skills which they use outside work at present. Many people in fairly mundane jobs turn out to have an amazing skills base; they may have excellent interpersonal skills which they use to coax volunteers to clean out canals, or be extremely good at chairing difficult meetings of the tenants' association, or use project planning techniques unknowingly to plan complex holiday itineraries.
- *Strategies*: We are now into the Action Plan stage of mentoring. How will the new ideas be implemented? What needs to be done, what steps are needed, how will progress be monitored? What help will the mentee need and where will such help be obtained? How will they avoid the traps that arise from our working styles? If we recognize any of these stress-related patterns, we need to check that the strategies are not influenced by the unhelpful aspects of their working styles (nor limited by personal or psychological styles).
- *Success*: Finally, what are the factors associated with success? Often we plan changes but fail to consider the impact on others—and they unwittingly (or deliberately) sabotage us because the changes are resented. How will the mentee change recognition patterns to be sure of support from colleagues, friends, managers? How will they maintain motivation if others try to talk them out of the changes?

Generating ideas

I have mentioned that our creativity seems to decline as we become adults. In reality, the same level of creative thinking is still available to us—we simply need the right circumstances to risk displaying it. Creativity techniques will help; the following are just a few suggestions:

■ *Brainstorming*: done properly! The activity called brainstorming in many organizations is a travesty. True brainstorming is more like a word association game. We call out, and capture on paper, anything that occurs to us. Comments by others are the triggers, and it is the way our subconscious mind operates that enables us to generate ideas that our conscious mind would reject too readily. There must be no censoring as otherwise we keep our ideas to ourselves (or get into conflict). There should be no discussion until after the brainstorming session has ended. Becoming rational too early will simply discourage the childlike, inner creative urge.

■ *Force-fitting*: Take a story that appears to have nothing to do with the situation under consideration. This might be a fairy story, a famous play or even a television programme. Have the mentee tell the story briefly, reviewing the key aspects and identifying the characters. Then have the mentee force-fit this story into the real world. The mentee takes the situation currently faced and tells it as if it were the same story. The characters in the story become the real people involved. By the time the mentee has struggled through this strange task, they will see things quite differently and should be able to generate new ideas.

■ *Fantasy excursion*: This also involves telling a story. However, now the mentee invents the story. Mentees can incorporate whatever they wish, so that their fantasy solutions can be included. For example, difficult people can have spells put on them, the mentee can become a superhuman alien and the organization can be converted into a holiday camp (unless it already is, in which case it can be changed into something else!) Again, the change in perspective will initiate new ways of proceeding.

Action planning and application

I have put action planning and application together because they are so closely interconnected. The quality of the action planning will determine the success or otherwise of the application. The application is done by the mentee alone, so it is important that the mentor prompts them to consider all likely snags when they are planning what to do. There are several ways of doing this, all involving some form of weighing up of pros and cons. A force-field analysis looks directly at the factors acting for and against a decision. We can consider the way in which beliefs and habits interfere with effective implementation; and guidelines for setting objectives will help to prevent the mentee from setting themself up for a case of self-sabotage.

Force-field analysis

The shift from alternatives into action planning requires a decision about which options to pursue. This may become obvious as a result of the SWOT analysis or working through the Steps to Success. If not, a force-field analysis may help. For this, the mentee prepares a sheet for each potential action, summarizing the forces working for and against achievement of that option. For example, a decision to change occupation might stimulate the following items in the force field:

FOR
- Enthusiasm for new type of work
- Will provide a challenge—current job is now too easy
- May become redundant anyway if I stay in current post
- Have attended training course for some of the skills required
- Plenty of support from family
- Family prepared to move to new location
- Company will pay relocation costs

AGAINST
- Lack several of the skills—would have to attend training programme in own time
- No good school at new location
- Have just finished decorating present home
- Estimate a frustrating few months before I would become competent enough to do the job without supervision

As with the SWOT, the items in the force-field analysis can be given a weighting so that an overall score can be calculated. If this is done, it will be important to include the 'soft' issues, such as how the mentee feels about the change, as well as the 'hard' factual data, such as the impact on salary. A force field which includes plenty of positive emotional responses to a change will be different from one where the only considerations are practical issues, such as money.

Objective setting

An action plan arising from a developmental alliance may represent a fairly substantial amount of 'work' to be done by the mentee. The plan will therefore need to be segmented in some way, with priorities allocated so that the mentee is not trying to change everything at once. Any technique for drawing up detailed action plans with specific goals and objectives will be useful.

For example, a first stage may be to convert what is probably a *hazy*[7] into a specific goal. This means taking what is probably a fairly vague wish and describing it in detail so that a clear outcome can be identified.

For example, the hazy: *to get a better job* translates for one mentee into:
- a job with more challenge and stimulation, so I enjoy going to work each day
- that pays at least 10 per cent more than my present job, so I can afford an annual holiday overseas
- a job that uses my specialist scientific training
- and that will enable me to attend professional conferences at company expense
- that will not require me to move house

Note: the mentor may need to help the mentee check the hazy for realism!

Once the hazy has been converted into a goal, this can be subdivided into a series of subgoals, which can in turn be further subdivided into objectives, and an action plan tree can be drawn as shown in Figure 8.6.

To increase the likelihood that mentees will achieve their objectives, and so that they will know when they have, each objective should meet guidelines such as RAW (realistic, attainable, worthwhile), or SMART

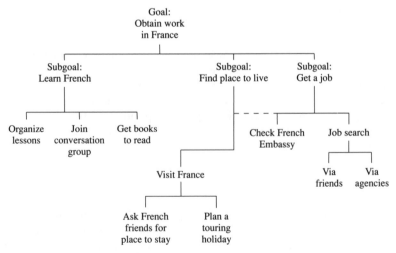

Figure 8.6 *An action plan tree.*

(specific, measurable, achievable, realistic, time-based), or the one I prefer, MMM (that comes with a bag of sweets!):

- *Measurable*: so that the end result is clear; so that the mentee gets the satisfaction of knowing that they have achieved the objective; so that the mentor also has a way of tracking and celebrating the success of the mentee.
- *Manageable*: so that the mentee can, in fact, achieve the objective; so that they do not set themselves up to fail while trying to do too much; so that they pick only actions they control themselves and not changes they wish other people would make.
- *Motivational*: so that they really want to achieve the objective; so that the benefits are obvious; so that the changes they make will have a positive impact on their future.

Appraisal

It is unlikely that the mentoring stages will be as neatly separated as I have described them in this book. In reality, the mentee will probably continue to recycle through the stages for different aspects. The support of the mentor for any action taken by the mentee will be particularly important. Watching progress will also be a form of reward for the mentor, who will now see the tangible results of personal mentoring skills.

An important part of any relationship is the way in which those involved review what happens between them. If this review includes open and constructive feedback, the relationship will continue to develop and improve. Something as significant as a developmental alliance will certainly need such a process.

The appraisal phase of the mentoring relationship has two main forms: appraising whether the mentoring is leading to the desired results for the mentee, and reviewing the mentoring relationship itself. For the *results* part of the appraisal, the focus will be on the content; for the *relationship* we need to consider the process.

Appraisal will also have two time structures: by session and over the longer term. Reviews at the end of each session can cover both content and process briefly, in a few minutes. Over the longer term it will be necessary to arrange specific meetings from time to time. Some of these will be normal mentoring sessions which come at the appraisal stage— i.e. after the mentee has activated the action plan and comes back to report on progress. Other meetings will need to be planned separately, specifically to review the ongoing relationship. Having definite appointments for these will make sure that this aspect does not get overlooked.

If both mentor and mentee become *very* skilled at conducting mentoring sessions, they *might* be able to switch between content and process. This would mean that they were comfortable changing the conversation instantly from mentee needs to mentor skills. If they do this, they will need to signal it clearly to each other. It is, in effect, changing the agenda at that point, and it will help if both do so at the same time!

The rest of this chapter consists of a checklist of aspects to cover during appraisals. For end-of-session reviews it will probably be enough to answer a single question for each item. For the longer review sessions I have given several areas to consider.

End-of-session reviews

- Did we have a good *contact* with each other?
- Was there a clear *contract* established?
- Was the *content* relevant to the mentee?
- How well were the *contrasts* between us dealt with and used?
- How well did we get on at a *personal* level?
- Were there any unhelpful *psychological* undercurrents?
- Did we both show *professional* skills as mentor and mentee?
- Have we checked for any *parallel* processes?
- Is a clear *aim* emerging for the mentee?
- Are new *alternatives* being generated for the mentee?
- Are ideas being turned into appropriate *actions*?
- Is the mentee increasing in *autonomy*?

Notes

1. A useful source of more information about the NLP technique for establishing rapport is Laborde, Genie Z., *Influencing with Integrity*, Syntony Publishing, 1987.
2. Rogers, Carl, *Client-Centred Therapy* , Constable & Co Ltd, 1951.
3. Tannen, Deborah, *You Just Don't Understand*, Virago Press, 1991.
4. Buzan, Tony, *Make the Most of Your Mind*, Pan Books, 1981.
5. Kelly, George, *The Psychology of Personal Constructs*, Norton, 1955. See also note 4, Chapter 2 for more references.
6. The idea of a genogram is taken from McGoldrick M. and Gerson R., *Genograms in Family Assessment*, Norton, 1985.
7. Hazies come from Jongeward, Dorothy and Seyer, Philip, *Choosing Success*, John Wiley & Sons Inc., 1978.

Checklist: Ongoing appraisal—C4P4A4

Contact

- Have we got a good connection?
- Are we in rapport with each other most of the time?
- How solid is the bond between us?
- Do we feel able to challenge each other when appropriate?
- Is our relationship deep enough for self-disclosure and sharing of feelings?

Contract

- Do we have clear contracts for each session and for the overall mentoring relationship?
- Have we considered the different levels of the contract—procedural, professional and psychological?
- Are we working within those contracts?
- Do we have the right parties involved in our contracts?

Note: this is about the quality of the contracting process rather than the specific content of the contract itself.

Content

- Is the content of our discussions relevant to the contract?
- Are we focusing on content that relates to the mentee and not the mentor?
- Are we satisfied that we understand each other's mind maps?
- Is the mentee organizing spot mentoring, training or other activities when more information is needed?

Note: again, this is about the way in which content is being dealt with rather than the detail of the content.

Contrast

- How are our similarities strengthening or weakening the mentoring?
- How are our differences strengthening or weakening the mentoring?
- How do we handle differences in beliefs and values?
- Is there an effective balance between support and challenge from the mentor?

Personal

- How well do we get on together?
- How do our psychological styles affect the mentoring process?

- How do our personal styles affect the mentoring process?
- How do our working styles affect the mentoring process?
- What is our time management like during the mentoring sessions?
- How do the mentee's learning styles affect the process?
- Are we *both* growing as a result of the relationship?

Psychological

- Are there dynamics affecting us at an unspoken level?
- Are we being completely open and honest with each other?
- What happens when we disagree?
- Are we avoiding getting into dependency mode?
- Is the mentor genuinely pleased when the mentee makes his/her own decision?
- Are we able to handle this review comfortably and honestly?

Professional

- What did the mentor do that was helpful?
- How did the mentee respond?
- What did the mentor do that was not helpful?
- How well is the mentor using skills of listening, questioning, reflecting, feedback, etc?
- What additional skills might the mentor develop for the future?
- Are we using models and frameworks that we both understand?

Parallel

- Have we checked for possible parallel processes?
- Are there any similarities in the way we are interacting and the way in which the mentee interacts with others?
- Or the way the mentor interacts with others?

Aim

- Is the mentee being helped to develop a clear vision for future direction?
- Are we using the information from the lifeline or SWOT analyses?
- Does the mentor recognize the aims of the mentee rather than impose what they think is best?
- Are we consistently working towards the goals of the mentee?

Note: as with contract and content, this is about the process of clarifying the aim rather than the detail of the aim itself.

Alternatives

■ Does the mentee have genuine new ways of viewing the situation?
■ Has the mentee been helped to identify alternative options?
■ Does the mentee have more strategies for achieving personal aspirations?
■ Are suggestions from the mentor presented tentatively so that the mentee is the decision maker?

Action

■ Has the mentoring included discussion of future actions?
■ Has the mentee been helped to plan action that they will be taking?
■ Are the actions carefully thought through?
■ Does the action plan take account of possible barriers?
■ Does the action plan include ways to reinforce and celebrate successes?

Note: process again rather than content—how the mentoring has enabled the mentee to draw up action plans, regardless of the content of those plans.

Autonomy

■ Has the mentoring enabled the mentee to become more autonomous?
■ Does the mentee accept responsibility for self-development?
■ Is the mentee confident about aiming for what they really want?
■ Is the mentee able to ask appropriately for what they want?
■ Do we need to plan for the ending of the mentoring relationship yet?
■ Have we celebrated achievements to date?

9 | The characteristics of mentors

There are a number of things to consider about any potential mentor. What follows is only an approximate order of priority. I have started with those aspects I consider to be most important, with less significant aspects left until later. However, I have not attempted to allocate first, second, third places. I believe that every mentee, and every mentor, needs to decide the final rankings for themselves.

We also have to recognize that human beings are human beings! No-one is going to score top marks on everything. No-one will be the perfect mentor. This is why I include a recommendation that mentors be committed to ongoing self-development. They will then be more likely to work with the mentee to increase the effectiveness of the mentoring relationship and to deal openly with any relationship difficulties.

One other point before you read on. I have mentioned some specific models for analysing things such as personal styles, thinking styles, working styles. Elsewhere in the book you will find similar ideas, including some frameworks for analysing an organization. *Any* models like this would do—so feel free to substitute those that you use already. I have included my choices more to illustrate the points than to imply that these are the best or the only ones worth considering.

Compatibility

The first thing to consider about any potential mentor must be whether they will be compatible with a mentee. Obviously this will depend also on specific mentees—there are, however, some traits that we can be fairly certain are needed by any mentor. The key elements are trust, respect and ethics.

Trust

Trust has to be high on the list of essential characteristics for a mentor. This applies in both directions—can they be trusted by a mentee, *and* will they in turn trust the mentee? This mutual trust is essential. Mentoring is a very significant, very intense relationship. Mentees will want to reveal their innermost worries—about their abilities, about their relationships, about their hopes and fantasies for the future. They will want to be sure that such confidences will not be betrayed. They will also find it easier, and more natural, to trust someone who makes it evident that they trust in return.

Mutual trust will also be enhanced when a mentor is willing to be open about their own shortcomings—hence the need for them to trust the mentee with this information. Mentors don't have to do this a lot—but enough for a mentee to connect with them as a fallible human being. No-one likes admitting their own mistakes to an irreproachable paragon.

How do we know whether someone can be trusted? We may be satisfied to rely on intuition—provided this has not let us down in the past. Otherwise we need to collect data. What do other people think of the mentor we have in mind? Can we find 'witnesses' prepared to vouch for them—people who are prepared to confirm that confidentiality has been maintained? Have we had previous contact with the person—if so, what happened to any information we gave? Are they in the kind of job where confidentiality and trust are expected—such as personnel officers who refer to staff records, technical staff who have access to secret new design details, managers who see sensitive commercial information?

Respect

Closely connected with trust is respect. Again, it is important that this is mutual—will the mentor respect the mentee and will the mentee respect the mentor? Respect is critical if you are to have a true developmental alliance between equals—the mentor must regard the mentee as a responsible adult and not as someone they have to take care of. That respect should therefore encompass the mentee's ability and right to think and decide for themself.

In turn, the mentee will need to respect the mentor, as an individual and as a professional. The mentee need not, however, be blind to the mentor's weaknesses—true respect is when we regard a person well even though we accept that they do not excel at everything; we respect that person 'warts and all'.

Another element of respect concerns understanding other people's views of the world. We each have our own frame of reference, or pattern of beliefs, which shapes how we interpret what goes on around us. Respect for another means respecting their personal map of the world. The American Indian recommendation, that you have to walk for a day in another person's moccasins before you can understand their point of view, is relevant here. Respect is the quality that means we are willing to step into their moccasins to find out.

There are any number of key issues over which people's opinions may differ, such as how people should be treated, what we think motivates us (e.g. money, friendship, prestige, fear), standards of behaviour, attitudes to timekeeping, whether organizations should provide staff training, how employee representation should be handled, and so on. The match, or otherwise, of opinions between mentor and mentee may have a significant impact on the level of mutual respect established.

Often, to find someone we will respect we first have to settle for someone whose views seem closest to our own. This is a natural step, although as we develop we can aim to increase our own level of tolerance for a range of opinions. Mentees may need time for this, though; it will not help them to be struggling with totally opposing opinions with their very first mentor. At the same time, it should not be made too easy—people will not be challenged to see things in new ways if they settle for the comfort of a mentor whose views are exactly the same as their own. They may also find it hard to respect a mentor who appears to have few firm views.

Ethics

Closely associated with respect is the question of ethics. Ethics might be defined as the way we behave in line with our values or opinions. This area is becoming increasingly significant in organizational life. Consider the following examples—how do you think individuals and organizations should be behaving in these areas:

- pollution control
- recycling
- equal opportunities
- health and safety
- tax avoidance
- working with the community
- trade with less developed areas of the world.

You can probably add a few of your own to the list. The key questions are: Where do potential mentors and mentees stand? How might these views affect a mentoring relationship? How will mentors (and mentees) be likely to deal with differences?

Qualities

Having assessed whether a mentor is likely to be reasonably compatible with an 'average' mentee, we now need to consider the qualities they need. These are self-awareness, a commitment to self-development, a positive attitude towards the concept of mentoring and a high tolerance of ambiguity.

Self-awareness

Self-awareness is essential if the mentor is not to use the mentee, unwittingly, as a substitute for themself. Rather like parents living vicariously through their children, there is a danger that mentors may re-live their own careers through their mentees. Mentors need to be conscious of their own motives, of the peaks and troughs of their own working lives, of their wishes and desires, so that they will not emit psychological undercurrents which invite their mentees into action replays—especially replays that conflict with the best interests of the mentee.

Another aspect of self-awareness concerns the mentor's knowledge of personal preferences, methods of working, motivation patterns, learning styles and so on. The mentor needs to recognize that they are not the mentee, that the mentee may well have very different styles and preferences, and that the mentee role is meant to function within the frame of reference of the mentee—the mentor is not there to turn out a clone of themself. Put simply, the mentor must be self-aware enough to keep personal 'stuff' separate from what is happening with/to the mentee.

Finally, the mentor needs enough self-awareness to avoid the traps of transference and projection. They must see the mentee as the mentee really is, in the here-and-now, and not project onto them some images from other people in the past. Mentors must also sidestep the way that some mentees will unknowingly attempt to transfer onto the mentor some aspects which really belong to other people who the mentee knew in the past. An everyday example of this occurs when mentees think they have found a 'father figure' (or 'mother figure') and mentors believe they are helping their own child (or themselves as a child!).

Self-development

Another key aspect to check is whether a prospective mentor is keen to self-develop. Someone who believes they can no longer change and grow is unlikely to spur others on. Do they have mentors of their own? How often do they attend training or development events? Are they in any professional associations or networks? Do they sometimes meet with other mentors to exchange ideas and support each other? Can they talk about the ways in which they have grown and developed over the years, and recently? Do they recognize that acting as a mentor will be developmental for them as well as for the mentee? Are they willing to learn alongside the mentee?

Attitude

Next we need to consider 'attitude'—a much over-used word for which the meaning has become blurred. I use it here to refer to our consistent beliefs which are demonstrated in our habitual actions. When we relate this to mentoring itself, the following are some of the questions we might ask:

- What is the potential mentor's attitude to other mentors, and to mentoring in general?
- Is the mentor in contact with other mentors, and do they treat them with professional respect?
- Does the mentor honestly think that mentoring is a valuable approach, or are they doing it purely to satisfy organizational expectations?
- What is that person's track record as a mentor?

We all have to start somewhere, but some mentors will already have helped others successfully. On the other hand, it may be better to 'grow new ones' if existing mentors will be too brainwashed into the traditional mentoring approach.

Ambiguity

Related to attitude will be the potential mentor's reaction to ambiguity. I hope I have already made it clear that we need a new approach to mentoring because the world is changing so rapidly. There are no right answers (maybe there never were, but at least people did not have to face that fact quite so directly in the past!).

It is no longer helpful for mentors to apply their own experiences to the situation of the mentee. Change has taken place at all levels—the task, the job, the ways in which we work with others, the structure of organizations, the market economy, and, of course, world politics. Within this maelstrom of change, individuals must, above all, be able to handle ambiguity. They must maintain their sense of comfort even when they have little idea what to do next.

This is difficult enough for a mentee to do—and the mentor must do it while also helping the mentee. The mentor thus gets a 'double dose' of the changes affecting them *and* the changes affecting the mentee. A high tolerance level is needed; mentors who think that the world is still predictable will not provide adequate support and challenge to their mentees.

Styles

The ways in which mentors handle ambiguity, and develop themselves, and behave in ways which lead others to trust and respect them, depend on the range of styles they have available. The more flexible they are, the more skilled they will be at interacting with a range of mentees.

There are many ways of classifying styles to help us understand people. Scientific models each explain different parts of the whole, although no one theory can explain everything. The *bootstrap*[1] theory proposes that we therefore select whichever theory seems most useful at the time.

I have selected a few here to show how we can apply them to increase our awareness of the mentoring relationship. I use some of the same frameworks in the next chapter when I focus specifically on the behaviour of the mentees. As I mentioned earlier, you could take your own favourite theories and apply them in the same ways.

Personal styles

Does the potential mentor have them all? By that, I mean do they have a full complement of personal styles? Observe the way in which mentors interact with a variety of people—do they change their approach to suit the individual or are they stuck in a 'behavioural rut'? We can identify five basic styles, which everyone uses in different amounts. Some of us stay locked into only one style; most of us can move between the five styles as the situation requires. We can be:

- controlling
- nurturing
- logical
- adaptable
- spontaneous

The best mentors have all five styles in good working order. They are able to be firm and controlling without becoming authoritarian and insisting that they are right. They can be nurturing and reassuring without being so caring that they smother people. They have a logical, rational style when there are problems to solve, but not so often that they seem more like a computer than a human being. They adapt and fit in with the reasonable expectations of others without being overly submissive or turning rebellious. And they are sometimes spontaneous, showing genuine friendliness and fun, as well as appropriate anger or sadness, without seeming immature or over-emotional.

It is not essential for someone to have an equal amount of each style, but it is important that they use each style sometimes. If mentors spend too much time in only one or two styles, they limit the ways in which mentees can interact with them. For example, too much controlling would leave a mentee with little option other than to adapt or become argumentative. Too much spontaneity, and the mentee becomes secretly (or overtly) critical. Too much nurturing is a common problem with mentoring—it leaves the mentee feeling stifled and unable to develop because the mentor insists on being over-protective.

Thinking styles

It is also worth checking any potential mentor's thinking styles. Our thinking styles influence the ways in which we solve problems and make decisions. The best decision makers have a balance between three modes of thinking. They blend opinions and experience from the past, emotional responses and reactions in the present, and logical consideration of the future impact of the decision. Less effective thinkers put too much weight on one or two modes only. Thus, some of us ignore past experience, some of us insist that feelings are irrelevant, while some of us seem unable to weigh up the facts rationally.

As shown in Figure 9.1, there are two more elements to consider during the thinking process—the event itself and the environment in which it occurs. Some of us react to events without paying enough attention to the context, so that we overlook significant considerations. We may thus decide on an action which will lead to unfortunate consequences. Alternatively, we may be so busy scanning the environment that we fail to notice what is actually happening right now.

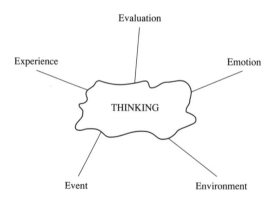

Figure 9.1   *Thinking styles.*

A mentor who fails to take account of all five strands may:

- rely too much on personal experience and expect the mentee to 'follow in their footsteps'
- appear inhumanly rational as they estimate probabilities and evaluate options without regard for any personal inclinations (or maybe they

give a weighting to the mentee's preferences that still fails to reflect the true strength of feeling involved)

■ get too emotionally involved in issues, so that the mentee has to cope with the mentor's anger, disappointment, ambition or other reaction—in which case the mentee may start to protect themself (or the mentor) by censoring what they share

■ focus solely on the current event and fail to fit it into the wider developmental context for the mentee. The mentor who does this is in danger of shifting into a counsellor role

■ insist on reviewing the environment in so much depth that nothing is ever resolved.

The best choice will be a mentor who balances and combines all three thinking modes, while taking full account of event and environment. However, failing that there could still be a useful combination between mentor and mentee. It will be important to avoid a pairing where both overlook the same aspects—they might feel like kindred spirits, but there will be omissions in the decision-making process and a lack of appropriate challenge from the mentor.

Working styles

We can add another bootstrap with a working styles framework. This time there are five again: unlike personal styles, most people tend to show strong indications of only one or two working styles. Each style has its pros and cons—the key is to choose a mentor who exhibits the strengths of the style without too many of the drawbacks.

■ Hurry Up   doing everything as quickly as possible
but
impatient, interrupt, make mistakes

■ Be Perfect   checking that work is totally accurate
but
nitpicking, critical, give too much detail

■ Please People   aiming to get approval from everyone
but
scared to challenge, sycophantic

■ Try Hard   enthusiastically having a go at anything
but
bore easily, don't finish what they start

■ Be Strong   staying calm under any amount of pressure
but
cold, unfeeling, won't ask for help

We can assess likely working styles by observing behaviour and by listening to sentence patterns. Hurry Ups are characterized by talking fast and interrupting; Be Perfects by careful grammar and use of long words; Please People make most of what they say sound like a question (in case you don't like it); Try Hards go off on tangents as they think of things while they're talking; and Be Strongs sound fairly monotonous and tend to call themselves 'one' (like the Royal Family).

Hurry Up mentors are likely to arrive late for mentoring appointments, get impatient and interrupt the mentee during the session, keep looking at their watch and probably want to finish early because they are already late for their next meeting. On the other hand, they may well impart a useful sense of urgency to a mentee, they will usually be willing to fit in an extra session at the last minute if the mentee has a crisis and they may even agree to mentor several people because they are good at finding time to get a lot done.

Be Perfect mentors like to do things properly. They will plan the mentoring process itself, start and finish sessions exactly on time, keep careful notes and stimulate the mentee to give careful consideration to the full range of factors affecting their development. Unfortunately, if they overdo this style the mentee will end up spending so long drawing up the 'perfect' development plan that the two of them grow old together before anything gets actioned!

Please People mentors may be reluctant to challenge their mentees in case they upset them, or they may discourage mentees from taking action in case they upset someone else, or they may flip to a parental stance and accuse the mentee of upsetting *them*. On good days, however, the Please People mentor will be sensitive and intuitive, picking up any signs of doubt or discomfort on the part of the mentee, demonstrating empathy and generally establishing a warm and close bond.

The *Try Hard* mentor's main strength is enthusiasm. These people will approach the role of mentor energetically, keen to cover all aspects. They are likely to encourage the mentee to get as much as possible from the process, including using spot mentors, experimenting with new approaches to mentoring and trying out new ideas between sessions. They will also prompt the mentee to apply the process to family and social life and not just to work. The danger here is that the mentee is encouraged to change on too many fronts at once. Try Hard mentors may generate ideas excessively—and may lose interest before actions have been successfully implemented. They may go off on tangents, raising so many suggestions that none is properly explored and evaluated.

Mentors who have a *Be Strong* style may appear remote and out of touch. Their tendency to act like a poker player makes it hard for mentees to get to know them. Their lack of emotional response discourages mentees from confiding in them; no-one wants to admit weaknesses or raise concerns with people who seem to have their own lives under so much control. A major advantage of Be Strong mentors, however, is their calmness. If a mentee does confide in them, they will react equally to even the most shocking revelations, making it easier for the mentee to discuss traumatic events. Mentors with this style will also be good at handling emotional outbursts from mentees, helping them to move on to practical problem solving once they have vented their feelings.

Practicalities

It is all very well to consider the styles, qualities and compatibility of mentors—but what if they don't have the time or the inclination? There are certain practicalities that must be taken into account! I include mentoring skills under this heading, too, as I believe that acquiring these is often simply a matter of finding the opportunity to learn and practise.

Resources

There are a number of items which I have grouped under a general heading of 'Resources'. What is needed from a mentor? Time is certainly on the list; there is no point in having a mentor who is going to cancel appointments or limit mentees to hasty sessions at long intervals. More time is needed for mentors to continue with their own professional development, to meet with their own mentors, to build up their mentoring skills and perhaps to review and discuss their mentoring 'caseload' when they need fresh insights.

There may also be a need for a place to meet—traditional mentors typically have (or used to have) offices, and secretaries to prevent interruptions. For developmental alliances between equals, a meeting place will still be needed, but it might be at the mentee's location or somewhere neutral.

Then there are particular skills that mentees might hope to learn from their mentors. Does the mentor require specific technical or professional knowledge? Would it be best if the mentor were in a certain part of the organization? Remember that we may not need these resources in a long-term mentor. Instead, it may be appropriate to identify a number of people who might be approached for *spot mentoring*. These individual sessions, with a particular focus, may generate information for subsequent discussion within a broader mentoring arrangement.

Contacts

Another cluster of factors are the contacts that the mentor is likely to have. Might they know anyone in the mentee's family or among the mentee's friends or colleagues? How might the mentee feel about such contacts? How might the family or friends feel about that person becoming the mentor? Does the mentor know the supervisor or manager? Again, how might the mentee feel about that? How might the mentee's manager react—will they try to get feedback from the mentor, or might they feel resentful? Does the mentor know other mentors? Could this lead to them exchanging information about a particular mentee? Would this be viewed as helpful or seen as a problem?

There are no right answers to these questions—often they can only be answered once a mentee is in contact with a specific mentor. What matters is that the implications are considered carefully so that they do not lead to problems later.

Mentoring skills

Most of the skills needed by a mentor are the same as those required in a range of interpersonal situations, so anyone who is reasonably successful at working with other people will have them. If not, it is not too difficult to acquire them as long as there are opportunities to learn and practise. The basic skills will be those of listening, questioning, reflecting and giving feedback.

Choosing a mentor

Having identified potential mentors, there is then the requirement to pair up specific mentors with specific mentees. The key factors include a decision on how closely the two should match each other, how well the mentor will challenge yet support a particular mentee and whether an element of role modelling is appropriate.

Mix and match

The 'mix and match' cluster includes a range of factors on which mentors and mentees might be matched, or where there might be benefits to being different. These factors are:

- *gender*: same or different sex mentor?
- *culture*: someone from the same cultural background, or someone who knows well the culture in which the mentee is planning to work?
- *education/qualifications*: same as the mentee, higher or lower?
- *background*: will social class make a difference, or what school or college they went to?
- *age*: would an age gap be a complication, can the mentor be younger than the mentee?

Support *and* challenge

Next, we need to consider what type of relationship particular pairs of mentors and mentees might have and what type they might want. Although there are stages in our learning when we need more support or more challenge, over a period of time we need both. Will the mentee be able to get both from the proposed mentor? What confirmation is there that the mentor has supported *and* challenged people in the past? Are there previous colleagues, junior staff, even previous mentees who can confirm this?

The balancing considerations mentioned previously in relation to styles will also be useful when considering support and challenge. For example, a mentor whose thinking style is strong on using past experience may be good at challenging a mentee who tends to reinvent the wheel. Or a nurturing personal style may be very helpful to support a mentee who lacks confidence and needs encouragement.

The working styles may also form the basis for support or challenge. Two Hurry Ups will be able to talk and work fast together—but may also make mistakes in the rush. A Be Perfect will add accuracy to a Hurry Up—but the strain of slowing down may lead to friction. Two Try Hards will share much enthusiasm—but may collude over not finishing the boring parts of the work. A Be Strong will prompt the Try Hard to be more conscientious—but the Be Strong's lack of feeling may depress the Try Hard.

Role model

Finally, it is worth considering whether a mentor needs also to be a role model and, if so, in what way. Will a mentee want to copy what the mentor does? Is the mentor likely to demonstrate ways of behaving which could usefully be added to the mentee's repertoire? This need not be restricted to management or leadership styles (although that may obviously be relevant). Role modelling includes anything we do—communicating with others, working in teams or alone, managing our time and our workload. Or we may benefit from seeing how someone else deals with organizational politics, with external pressures, or with particularly difficult situations.

Think about small children practising to be adults by copying what the grown-ups do. The same process works for us—we learn to be employees by copying other employees, supervisors by copying supervisors and so on. Just like children, we are at the mercy of the models with which we come into contact. An absence of good models means that we struggle to acquire effective behaviours.

Consider the areas in which a role model might be of help. We do not want to start the cloning process, but there are bound to be some areas in which mentees may have seen only mediocre performances by others. Consider whether the intended mentor will be a suitable role model to fill some of the gaps. At the very least, they will hopefully be a role model of a good mentor, so that the mentee can continue the pattern.

Notes

1. Chew, G. F. 'Bootstrap: A Scientific Idea?', in *Science*, 161, pages 762–65, 1968.

Checklist: A mentor 'application form'

The following is a tongue-in-cheek version of an application form to be completed by a mentor candidate!

Name

Age

Gender

Ethnic origin

Education

Examinations/Qualifications

Work history: Please show *all* employment, including paper rounds, Saturday jobs, vacation work, etc. Include also voluntary activities

Social activities, hobbies, spare-time interests

Training and development undertaken

Achievements: What do you regard as your most significant achievements?

Problems: What are the most significant problems you have encountered? What happened?

Strengths: What are your strengths? (*note*: not just at work)

Weaknesses: What are your weaknesses?

Experience: What is your experience of being mentored? of providing mentoring?

Expectations: What do you think a mentor does or should do? What do you expect of becoming a mentor?

Motives: What prompts you to become a mentor? What do you expect to get out of it for you?

Interpreting the responses

Some of these headings are obvious, e.g. age, education, etc.; these will help you to mix or match. Under the Training and Development heading, you can see whether the prospective mentor continues to be open to learning on a regular basis, as well as whether they have already attended mentoring or similar interpersonal skills courses.

The *way* in which 'candidates' complete the 'application' yields clues to their working styles. Hurry Ups write briefly and hand in the form at the last minute. Be Perfects complete it beautifully and include the exact dates and the address of the shop where they did their paper round. Please People do their best to guess what you want to hear and say they hope it's all right when they hand it in (or add a little note to that effect). Try Hards go off on tangents in response to the questions—and then don't complete their responses. And Be Strongs give nothing away but the facts!

The Achievements and Problems sections provide data about abilities to get on with people, to handle change and ambiguity, about whether they are likely to be respected and trusted, and to respect and trust others, and so on. For instance, if their significant problems are all caused by someone else, and their significant achievements are all achieved unaided, you might suspect their ability to make a significant connection with other mortals.

The way they respond to the questions on Strengths and Weaknesses will give you an idea of their level of self-awareness. Beware the people who have only strengths—and the ones who proudly announce lots of weaknesses.

Finally, if you add space for their address and where they engage in social activities, you may even be able to guard against mentor and mentee knowing the same people!

10 Understanding mentees

There are various frameworks and theories we could use to understand mentees (or mentors, or people in general for that matter). As I wrote in the previous chapter, which framework we use is not the most important factor. What matters far more is how well we are able to apply the framework. The best researched theories are not much help if we fail to use them competently.

To build on the previous chapter, I will repeat two of the models I used there but with examples from the perspective of analysing a mentee rather than a mentor. I will, however, begin the chapter with an additional framework and end it with one that pulls together several strands. Each of the frameworks I use are well-known in other contexts, and you may choose to skip this chapter if you are already familiar with them. However, I include them here because I have not seen them related specifically to the mentoring process before.

In addition to their use for planning a mentoring scheme, matching mentors and mentees, and so on, these frameworks will also be appropriate for the third stage in the developmental alliance. Mentors and mentees can use them as ways of analysing the trends experienced by the mentee. However, it will be crucial at that stage for these frameworks to be used sensitively. The purpose of having a theory is to help us understand what is happening, so that we can make good choices about what to do next; it is not so that the mentor can impress the mentee with knowledge. Use of the framework should therefore be either shared or silent. Shared use requires both parties to know the model in use and to jointly work out how it applies, while silent use means that the mentor works with the model in her or his head, to generate ideas which they put forward only tentatively.

Psychological styles

Psychological styles is my label for models such as the Myers-Briggs Type Inventory (MBTI)[1], which gives us a framework for classifying people into 16 types, based on preferences relating to their focus of attention, the way they take in information, their decision-making process and how they relate to the world. Although the full 16-type taxonomy is probably too complex for the layperson to remember, the basic four dimensions provide a much more accessible way of understanding how human beings manage to seem so different from each other. The values base to the MBTI is also excellent for mentoring as it reinforces the belief that diversity and difference are natural and should be honoured.

Extraversion/Introversion

This dimension should not be confused with the everyday misuse of the labels 'extroversion' and 'introversion'. In MBTI it refers to our focus of attention—is it to our inner or our outer world? It *may* relate to whether we dance on tables or behave like hermits but there are many more subtle shadings than this.

Extraverts are energized by the outer world. They like contact with people, a variety of activities, something going on. They are the people who enjoy telephone calls rather than seeing them as interruptions, who go to visit people rather than sending a memo—and are often oblivious to the fact that others may not welcome the intrusion.

Extraverts may therefore appear to be more enthusiastic than introverts about the mentoring process. They are likely to be networking already, will happily spend time with yet another person and will probably identify regular *spot mentors* as well. In their contacts with the mentor, they are also likely to focus on relationships and people skills as areas in which they wish to develop.

If problems arise, it may be because the mentor is more introvert and feels that the mentee is too demanding of personal time. A mentor with a shaky sense of self-worth may also feel threatened by the number of alternative mentors that are being involved. The mentor may also experience difficulty in getting the mentee to focus on areas not directly related to people, such as the 'technical' aspects of work.

Introvert mentees, on the other hand, will be delighted to concentrate on concepts and ideas, possibly to the detriment of their people skills. Introverts focus on their inner world—on what is going on inside them. They will enjoy having a mentor with whom they can discuss their thoughts and feelings, but may not be quite so interested when it comes to considering their relationships with other people.

Introverts are more likely to put things in writing, to spend time keeping a log or journal of their mentoring experiences, to draw up mini-agendas for their mentoring sessions. They will probably keep strictly to appointments and are unlikely to make contact with their mentors in between the timetabled sessions.

Although introverts may need more persuasion than extraverts to become mentees (or mentors) in the first place, they may go on to become more thoughtful and committed mentees in the end.

Sensing/Intuitive

The sensing/intuitive dimension relates to the ways in which we all take in information from the outer world. Even introverts have to exist in the outer world, so either of these approaches may be used by extraverts or introverts.

Sensors notice what is actually there. Intuitives 'see' what might be there. Sensors will come to mentoring with information about factual matters such as what requirements are written into job advertisements, the content of procedures manuals, the numbers of people employed and their grades and the locations of various departments and functions of the organization. Intuitives will seem to overlook the 'facts' and come to mentoring sessions expecting to review possibilities. They notice the potential links between separate situations, the opportunities that might be there and the ways in which they might progress their own development.

Sensors will seem grounded in reality, but may fail to spot genuine opportunities for development. Intuitives, on the other hand, may seize any number of opportunities, but may neglect to sort out the practicalities of their ideas before implementing them. If mentor and mentee match, the result may be too much practicality or too much chasing of vague possibilities—and if both are intuitives they may actually argue about which imagined possibilities are best! If mentor and mentee are too far apart, they may find it hard to reconcile their different perspectives on the world.

Thinking/Feeling

This dimension concerns the ways in which we make decisions. Thinkers do so based on logic; feelers take into account their own and others' feelings. Thinkers will be rational, using cause-and-effect sequences to come to a conclusion; feelers will be values-based, influenced by their own emotions and considering the impact on people of any decisions.

Thinking mentees are likely to select (if given the chance) a mentor who is logically a good choice—perhaps someone who is well situated to provide practical help, someone who is already known as an experienced and successful mentor, or the person who scores highest against a checklist of mentor qualities.

Such mentees will also expect to have rational discussions with their mentors. These may relate to the extraversion/introversion dimension, when they consider either the inner or the outer world, or be based on sensing/intuitive preferences to incorporate the facts or the opportunities.

Whichever of these it is, the main focus will be on the logic of any conclusions that are drawn.

Feeling mentees, by contrast, may well choose their mentors based on 'gut feeling'. It will be important for them that their selection feels right. They will also be concerned that the mentor holds similar values and beliefs to their own. They may link their own comfort to their faith in the mentor—this may mean finding one who is highly regarded by others, but could also be the impetus to trust someone who has never mentored before 'because their heart is in the right place'.

When making decisions, feeling mentees will want to talk openly about their own emotions and those of the mentor. Self-disclosure by the mentor will be appreciated, as will the chance to discuss fully the potential reactions of anyone likely to become aware of the actions taken by the mentee—and especially anyone likely to be affected by them. Harmony may well be a key concept.

Judging/Perceiving

The judging/perceiving scale refers to the way in which we deal with the external world. Judgers like to make decisions; perceivers prefer to keep their options open. Judgers therefore tend to live in a fairly structured way, while perceivers 'go with the flow'.

Judging mentees will want a structured approach to mentoring, with a fixed schedule of appointments. They are also likely to appreciate working through distinct stages of mentoring, so that they can plan ahead. The same trend will appear in the content of the mentoring—they will prefer to deal with issues and make decisions as they go along.

Perceivers, on the other hand, will tend towards more casual arrangements. They may be content to make appointments on a one-off basis, planning the next as they finish a session rather than having several in the diary in advance. They will also be more likely to want to rearrange appointments because something else has come up—and will accept the same behaviour from their mentor.

Perceivers have a habit of changing their minds when they obtain more information. They can also usually see more than one point of view. Applied to the content of their mentoring sessions, this will seem eminently sensible to a mentor who is also perceiving—and infuriatingly indecisive to a judging mentor!

Personal styles

In the previous chapter I mentioned that we each have available to us five different personal styles, or ways of behaving. I called them *controlling*, *nurturing, logical, adaptable* and *spontaneous*. You may have recognized *transactional analysis* (TA) as the source of these. They are from one of the TA models of *ego states*[2]—collections of feelings, thoughts and behaviours that show up in recognizable patterns. A more correct set of labels is:

> Controlling Parent
> Nurturing Parent
> Functional Adult
> Adapted Child
> Natural Child

Note that we do not have to be real parents, real adults or real children—the labels relate more to the ways in which we develop the behaviour patterns, as you will see in a moment. Most of us use the whole range, shifting to suit the circumstances. Sometimes a person seems stuck in a particular mode, such as the permanent Controlling Parent who tells everyone what to do, or the excessive Functional Adult who analyses everything—including jokes! The more we use all ego states, the better we are able to communicate effectively with a wide range of people.

The two Parent ego states are so-called because these are patterns that we learn as children by copying our parents or other caregivers. Real parents look after us by controlling and nurturing. When controlling they make sure that we know what the rules are ('Time for bed!'); when nurturing they encourage and reassure us ('You can do it'). Overly controlling parents may insist on rules for everything; over-nurturing parents may spoil us and fuss over us. In the world of grown-ups, in organizations, these ego states become the styles we use to be firm and let people know what is expected of them; and to be caring and encouraging, particularly when people face a challenge.

The two Child ego states refer to patterns that we develop for ourselves as we grow up. We start with natural, spontaneous behaviour; as grown-ups this translates into our ability to let others see how we really feel. Our genuine friendliness, our fun and our creativity all show via this ego state. So do authentic anger and sadness. Our Adapted Child, on the other hand, consists of behaviours learned in order to fit in with the expectations of society. So we restrained our natural impulses at times and learned to be polite, courteous, hold open doors, dress acceptably and so on. Provided that we don't overdo our adaptation, this ego state enables us to get along with other people. When we over-use our Child ego states, we come across as over-emotional and childish if we always show our feelings; submissive, withdrawn or rebellious if we don't get the level of adaptation in balance.

Our Functional Adult makes up the set of five. In this mode we behave logically and rationally. We collect information, weigh up pros and cons and make reasoned decisions. We can still overdo it—too much rationality makes us seem like unfeeling, inhuman computers. However, Functional Adult is invaluable when we need to engage in joint problem solving. We may also utilize it internally, to select an outward appearance of one of the other ego states—for example, when we make a conscious decision to be polite (Adapted Child) to an obnoxious colleague instead of being tempted to become judgemental (Controlling Parent) and insisting that they 'say please nicely'.

Let's look now at some examples demonstrating how a knowledge of ego states can be of use in mentoring.

Susan was a mentee who had firm opinions on most things, and made sure that other people knew them. In her work in the emergency services, her readiness to tell people what to do was generally an asset. She would arrive at an incident and take charge; in most cases people would follow her lead and the situation would be dealt with efficiently.

Unfortunately, Susan used the same style when there was no emergency. She was a team leader, and was finding that her team members were becoming almost mutinous when she held meetings. They complained that she treated them as if they were children. Susan confided in her mentor that her junior staff were difficult to supervise, that her manager failed to appreciate her skills at dealing with emergencies, and that a promotion had gone to a colleague who, in Susan's eyes, was weak and took too much notice of other people's opinions.

The mentor, Mike, suspected that Susan spent much of her time in Controlling Parent ego state. Mike realized that he, too, often felt as if Susan were talking down to him. He also guessed that, if he told Susan this, she would probably just tell him he was wrong!

Mike therefore suggested that Susan start a log of how she behaved and what results she got in different situations. He recommended some books for Susan to read, and encouraged her to ask for a place on a company training course on supervisory skills. Mike made a point of using extra Nurturing Parent with Susan, so that she would not be tempted to argue or try to out-control.

Another mentee, Harry, rarely used Controlling Parent, or, indeed, any ego state except Natural Child. In mentoring sessions, Harry was very open and let the mentor know exactly how he felt—about the mentoring and about what happened at work and at home. Brian, Harry's mentor, found it difficult to get Harry to discuss things in a logical way; Harry seemed to have few opinions and got upset easily. Brian felt drawn into spending a lot of the time in Nurturing Parent, comforting Harry, or Controlling Parent, feeling annoyed with Harry for being childish.

Brian therefore concentrated on using more Functional Adult. He persevered with asking Harry questions which needed a reasoned response. He showed Harry techniques for structured decision making. By being more in Functional Adult ego state himself, Brian gradually got Harry to start behaving in a similar way. Once Harry was doing this during the mentoring sessions, Brian was able to start a rational discussion about the effect of Harry's behaviour. He was also able to introduce the idea of Harry practising to use a wider range of ego states generally.

Working styles

I also referred in Chapter 9 to another five characteristic styles, this time classifying the way in which we work. These were: Hurry Up, Be Perfect, Please People, Try Hard, Be Strong. The working styles show up in the ways we do things, the ways we talk and the ways in which we are influenced to put energy into a task. The descriptions I give here are extreme examples; most people will show some of the signs, but few will fit the stereotype exactly. Often we have one style which we adopt the most, a second which we also use quite often, and then, occasionally, touches from the others.

However, our working styles show up far more when we are under stress—as may well be the case during mentoring sessions, particularly in the early days. Having already shown how this may affect the way in which mentors function, I will now describe some of the pitfalls facing mentees.

Hurry Up

People with Hurry Up style like to do everything as quickly as they can. This means that they get a lot done. They are energized by having deadlines to meet, and they always seem able to fit in extra tasks. Occasionally they go too fast and make mistakes, which can lose them time while they correct themselves. If they become stressed, they seem to go faster and faster and only make themselves more stressed. Hurry Ups think fast and talk fast. They are therefore quick to come up with solutions to problems, and can appear impatient with people who want to move more slowly, especially when they interrupt and want to do everything at once.

In a mentoring setting, Hurry Ups may want to rush things. They want an instant relationship, without taking time to get to know their mentoring partner. Then they can't see why there is a need to have so many stages in the mentoring process—why can't they go straight to the action stage? Even their action plans may be filled with lots of activities to be done in a very short space of time. They are also likely to report that their careers are not progressing as fast as they should. They may complain that people are slow or lazy—compared to their own frenetic pace a normal working speed may well seem inadequate to them.

Hurry Up mentees need to be reminded often that they can take their time. They need reassurance that the mentor will not rush away and does not expect instant results. The mentor can also help by encouraging the mentee to consider carefully before making decisions, and then giving praise when they do slow down in this way. Learning to do this with the mentor will be good practice for other situations.

Be Perfect

Be Perfect people are energized by doing things right. They aim for perfection in everything, and can therefore be relied upon to check carefully, produce accurate work and set high standards. Sometimes they will miss deadlines because they are still checking their work. They are reluctant to issue anything in draft format, preferring to keep at it until they judge it cannot be improved. This prevents other people from contributing to the task. They may also have a weak sense of priorities and insist that everything is done perfectly, so that they come over as overly critical 'nitpickers'.

When being mentored, Be Perfects set very high standards for themselves and may get discouraged if they fail to live up to their own high expectations. They may also lose faith in a mentor who makes a mistake, as they make little allowance for human failings. They will find it hard to take risks or try anything that does not guarantee perfect results. Be Perfects are likely to draw up detailed, well organized action plans; this is because they will have considered thoroughly what might happen in the future and allowed for it in their calculations.

What Be Perfects need is permission to make mistakes sometimes. They need to learn that 'to err is human'; otherwise they will continue to give themselves, and others, a hard time over even trivial errors. They will also need help from their mentor in coming to terms with the need to be flexible. Organizations are changing so much nowadays that it is impossible to set out rigid plans in advance. While attention to quality is obviously desirable, the Be Perfect also needs to develop the ability to live with some ambiguity.

Please People

Those with a Please People style like to get on with everyone. They are energized by the thought of approval and harmony. They make good team members because they involve others as a way of making sure that the others are happy. Please People are the ones who use their intuition to pick up when someone has doubts; they notice the little signs and the body language which others may ignore. On the other hand, they may be reluctant to challenge anyone in case they lose that person's approval. This may mean that they allow bad ideas to be implemented, or that they end up with too much to do because they 'couldn't say no'.

Please People may worry too much about having the approval of their mentor. They may attempt to read the mentor's mind and then say whatever they think the mentor wants to hear. They are likely to report being misunderstood at work—they do their best and people don't appreciate it. This will be because they guess how to be helpful, instead of asking outright. When they talk, they may make everything sound like a question so that they can quickly back down if their suggestions don't meet with instant agreement.

The mentor may have to limit the amount of approval they offer. It may be helpful to start with this so that the mentee relaxes, but there is a real risk that the mentor will end up making all the decisions. Because Please People find it painful to accept criticism, there is also a danger that the mentor will be tempted to restrict the feedback they give. Please People mentees need to be helped to see that someone's opinion of their behaviour is not automatically tied to whether the person likes them or not. These mentees also need to learn that people will respect them more if they sometimes voice their own opinions.

Try Hard

Try Hard people are enthusiastic, get involved in lots of different activities and tend to volunteer for things. They are energized by having something new to try. Sometimes they turn small jobs into major projects because they are so enthusiastic at following up every angle. However, they may then become bored with the detailed work that follows, even to the point of leaving work undone so that they can move on to another exciting new activity. When they talk, they have a habit of going off on tangents, so that their sentences run from subject to subject without a proper ending.

Try Hards are likely to be very enthusiastic mentees to start with. They will be keen to try out the various aspects of the mentoring process and may even introduce ideas and activities to the mentoring. However, their enthusiasm may not translate into action. They may start several initiatives, but then become bored and not finish any of them. Their descriptions of their work are likely to include plenty of exciting new projects but little mention of completion. They may be leaving the routine work for others to do, with corresponding damage to good working relationships as people begin to resent this.

These mentees will need a mentor who is firm about holding them to their commitments. Try Hards need to learn that putting effort into something is not enough—we also have to complete the task. The mentor should reinforce each act of completion with plenty of praise, so that the mentee realizes it can be just as satisfying to finish the job as it is to move on to something different. The mentor will need to beware of falling under the spell of the Try Hard's enthusiasm. It can seem almost churlish to insist that the routine work is done when there are exciting new prospects to tackle—but that is what is needed.

Be Strong

People with Be Strong working style pride themselves on their ability to stay calm in any circumstance. They are energized by the need to cope. They are good at dealing with crises, can handle difficult people and will work steadily through any workload. However, their desire to have everything under control means that they can come across as aloof and unfeeling. They are also reluctant to ask for help, even when they should. They may hide work away so that the manager thinks it has been taken care of. Their lack of awareness of emotions may make them insensitive to the feelings of others.

Be Strong mentees may find it hard to accept any help from the mentor. Even talking about problems may be difficult, as Be Strongs are reluctant to admit to any weaknesses, even to themselves. They may restrict the mentoring discussions to 'safe' factual topics and find it hard to share how they feel. Although they may be performing well in pressured situations at work, they may lack interpersonal skills. Although noted for being conscientious, they may appear to be inflexible because they tackle tasks as they arise, instead of taking account of people's requests for priority.

The mentor may have to guard against feeling superfluous. They will need to look behind the Be Strong mentee's apparent self-sufficiency and remember that we can all be helped by others. The mentor's perspective will be valuable in prompting the mentee to accept that organizations run on people contact—mentees can't afford to ignore the feelings of others just because their own responses are so unemotional. These mentees also need encouragement to ask for, and accept, help so that they learn not to do everything for themselves.

Combinations

It doesn't take long to realize that combinations of mentor and mentee working styles will work well, *provided* the positive aspects are maintained. For instance, a Hurry Up will add a consciousness of timescales to a Be Perfect who might otherwise take too long checking the work. A Please People can teach a Be Strong how to take notice of other people's reactions. A Try Hard will inject enthusiasm into what might otherwise be a monotonous approach from a Be Strong. A Be Strong can model how to stay calm for a Hurry Up who tends to rush about in a panic.

Of course, the results may not be quite so constructive if the *negative* aspects come to the fore. In that case, it may seem impossible to get a real connection between mentor and mentee. The Hurry Up then seems merely impatient, the Be Perfect hypercritical, the Please People ingratiatingly subservient, the Try Hard out of touch with reality and the Be Strong boringly predictable.

Motivation

I mentioned above that people are energized by different things, depending on their psychological or working style. Being energized is part of being motivated. The other part of motivation is recognition. All human beings need a certain amount of recognition from other human beings. Without it, we wither away, psychologically and physically. That is why solitary confinement is used as a punishment; only the strongest minded can survive for long periods without human contact.

Any way in which one person acknowledges another is a form of recognition. A glance, a handshake, a conversation, a hug ... these are all recognition in varying degrees of intensity. Negative recognition may be a scowl, an unfriendly comment, destructive criticism, a slap ...

Although we are not conscious of it, most of us have a pattern of recognition that feels right to us—an arrangement which seems to exist between us and others, within which we give and receive recognition. With some people there appears to be a one-way trade. For example, managers may compliment or criticize more junior staff, but some of the latter would hesitate to do the same back. With other people we may operate on a sort of exchange basis, where we swap 'recognitions', or *strokes*[3] as they are often called. This is what happens when we respond to a compliment with another compliment : 'That's a nice suit.' 'Thanks, and I really like your shoes.'

We can link recognition to working styles in order to better understand the motivation of mentees. Hurry Ups expect praise for being quick, Be Perfects like recognition for being accurate, and so on. We tend to give the kind of recognition we like to receive ourselves, so we don't always hit the target. For instance, if you're a Try Hard and comment on how enthusiastic a Be Strong is, they will probably be puzzled. Be Strongs will be much more comfortable with strokes about their calmness under pressure.

Checking mentee against mentor preferences is also useful. Does the mentor encourage the mentee to take responsibility for self-development, or might they inadvertently reinforce dependency on the mentor? A healthy mentoring recognition pattern will:

- reinforce the mentee's commitment to self-development
- include strokes in both directions: from mentor to mentee and vice versa
- have separate instances of strokes in each direction (no automatic swapping)
- focus on the positive—'what you stroke is what you get'
- start from what matters most to the mentee
- move on so that the mentee learns to accept a wider range of stroke formats
- involve practice for the mentee in giving a wider variety of strokes to others.

Combining the models

We can use a model developed by Taibi Kahler[4] to pull together some of the different models in this chapter. The alliteration is mine—so once again feel free to change the labels if you don't like memory aids that rely on the alphabet.

Taibi calls this an assessing quadrant and I have changed his terminology so that I can refer to it as AP: Active/Passive, Alone/People^2. It gives us a way of collecting together the clues about a person and slotting them into a particular 'box'.

Now, we all know that you cannot fit real human beings into neat little boxes. However, provided we keep this in mind it can still be quite helpful to use a set of boxes as the basis for an approximate sorting process. If we then make a point of being cautious in our conclusions, and tentative in our behaviour towards the person, we may well find that the sorting process does generate some useful ideas and options. The extra insight will usually enable us to interact more effectively right from the start.

We can, of course, use the same framework to analyse ourselves—and then apply the 'platinum rule', which is one on from the golden rule of 'do unto others as you would be done by'. The platinum rule says 'do unto others as *they* would be done by'. Knowing our own position on the quadrant allows us to guard against treating everyone else as if they have the same preferences.

Figure 10.1 AP^2.

The diagram in Figure 10.1 has two axes. The vertical axis refers to whether we act or react; the horizontal to our preferences for being alone or in a group.

It helps to bring this model to life if we take an example of someone arriving at an event at work that has both social and business connotations—perhaps an annual conference where employees are expected to mingle and socialize, but where they will also sit through presentations about the state of the business or long-term corporate plans and strategies. This type of setting allows us to identify how people prefer to interact, as they will have several options.

The same patterns will be evident if mentees are invited to a 'meet the mentors' event. Indeed, the patterns may be even more pronounced because the level of stress may be higher—will I find a suitable mentor, what happens if no-one wants to mentor me? And other worrying thoughts .... Under stress, we tend to do more of the same so mentees may well lock into, and therefore exaggerate, their preferred styles.

There will be fewer behavioural options open to a mentee who comes first for a one-to-one session with a new mentor. Such a setting means that we have no information about how the mentee reacts to groups. However, there are still several other indicators which can be used as clues in such situations.

As you read on, you will realize that the people I describe are caricatures. They are gross simplifications used to make the model clearer. However, having taught this material over many years, I know that these extremes are still recognizable—and that you will be able to use them to understand the underlying patterns involved.

Active/Alone

Those in the top right-hand box of the quadrant are active, so they initiate contact and their preference is to work alone or with only one or two people. Typically, therefore, they will go up to an individual (or maybe two already together) and start a conversation about work.

Kahler has identified that many of these people will wear neat, classic, business clothes—through choice rather than because it's expected; they may look just the same on their day off!

They may well have horizontal frown lines, and their speech tends to be precise and grammatically correct. They will not use slang, will pause as if for punctuation at the correct points and use long words because these are generally more specific than shorter, more everyday words. They sometimes add clauses as if in brackets (which they would call parentheses) into their sentences as, for example, I have done in this sentence.

Active/Alones are most comfortable with a Functional Adult–Functional Adult channel of communication. Their working style is likely to be Be Perfect and they will prefer that any recognition, or strokes, relates to their performance.

Mentees who fit this quadrant are likely to initiate conversation with their mentor as they arrive, and to focus immediately on the purpose of the meeting—i.e. mentoring and what they want to achieve. They will respond best to a mentor who is willing to discuss matters rationally and in some detail. They particularly enjoy the one-to-one nature of mentoring.

Active/People

Those in the top left-hand box are also active, so they, too, initiate conversations. However, they prefer to be with a group of people. They are therefore likely to approach a group and instantly become the focus of attention. There will then be plenty of mutual nurturing as they talk about family, friends, appearance and other non-work-related matters.

Kahler suggests that these people can be identified by their propensity to wear bright colours, jewellery and perfume. Women may feel they have more scope for this, whereas men may feel constrained to wear dark suits at work. In that case, they may still choose bright ties or braces, wear cufflinks, identity bracelets and aftershave!

Active/People are usually smiling, sometimes rather anxiously, and may also raise their eyebrows, often in a quizzical way. This may be accompanied by a tendency to phrase most comments as questions, as if they don't want to offend anyone by being too definite in their views. Their speech may be littered with 'weasel words'—such as 'sort of', 'you know', 'maybe', 'like'—which reduce the potency of their comments.

They tend to use a Nurturing Parent–Natural Child channel, switching from side to side depending on aspects such as organizational status, age, gender and content of each conversation. Their working style is most likely to be Please People and they much prefer their strokes to be about them as a person.

They will appreciate a mentor who makes time to get to know them as a human being, and may resent one who focuses too abruptly on getting down to business. They also expect to be nurtured and will appreciate encouragement from their mentor. Because they tend to nurture others, they will show a friendly interest in their mentor which goes beyond the developmental alliance itself.

Passive/People

Coming now to the bottom right, we have the people who opt for a group but are passive. They therefore move towards a promising looking group but do not instantly join it. Instead, they hover on the edges and wait for someone to draw them in. They are happiest talking about non-work matters such as hobbies and spare-time activities. Extreme versions of this 'type' may well move rapidly between interests so that it becomes hard to keep up with their progression through a series of new hobbies.

Kahler tells us that these people wear 'unusual' outfits. They may be the first to pick up on new fashions, discarding them once everyone else starts to wear the same. In organizations with strict dress codes, they may bend the rules, e.g. sandals with a business suit, or a novelty tie.

Passive/People are likely to have vertical frown lines in the centre of the forehead and may spend a lot of time making these deeper as they struggle to understand, to remember something, or to think of what they want to say. Their sentences may jump from subject to subject, going off on tangents and then trailing off without a proper ending. They use the word 'try' frequently.

They most enjoy a channel of Natural Child–Natural Child, in which they and their listeners display excitement and enthusiasm for the current topic. Their working style may well be Try Hard, and they will respond best to strokes about their 'play'—the range of hobbies and interesting new projects between which they move.

They prefer a mentor who shows an active interest in their non-work activities, and respond well to a playful approach. Teasing can be a useful way of confronting their tendency towards the 'butterfly-mind' syndrome.

Passive/Alone

In the bottom right are the people who would rather not attend the event at all. They prefer to be alone, and are passive so they do not initiate contact. Given the chance, they will stay away and work steadily on their own. Forced to attend, they will wait for someone to start talking to them.

According to Kahler, they will not show much interest in their appearance, so may arrive at work inappropriately dressed if there is no Controlling Parent at home to see to this for them!

Passive/Alones have smooth faces, with no worry or laughter lines. When they smile with their mouth it may not extend to their eyes. Occasionally someone with this style may be very jovial, although you may realize that the jokes are actually a defence against getting close. More often, they will appear stoic, and will speak in a monotone as if events are not connected to them.

They prefer Controlling Parent–Adapted Child communications; tell them to do something and they will respond. Their working style is most likely to be Be Strong, and they will probably appear uncomfortable if they are offered more than the occasional stroke. They are likely to respond that they are 'simply doing their job'.

They will expect the mentor to take charge and issue clear instructions, and react uncomfortably to any show of interest in their personal lives. The mentor will need to remind them that this is a mentoring and not a management arrangement. They are unlikely to seek out a developmental alliance, believing that they should be able to cope alone.

The third dimension

The assessing quadrant really needs to be drawn in 3-D to pick up the fifth working style. This is the Hurry Up mode, which seems to apply to any of the quadrants. There is a tendency for it to be seen more often in association with the two left-hand boxes, but this is not always the case.

People with this third dimension style will rush into the event, hurry across to an individual or a group, interrupt or behave in an agitated way until people speak to them, and then talk fast, interrupt others and finally rush away again.

I find it easier to work with the four boxes as described above and then to overlay the additional dimension when necessary. Thus, many people will not exhibit the Hurry Up style anyway. For those who do, the same communication channels will apply, but they will need to be used 'at speed'.

Hurry Up people will prefer recognition of their high level of productivity, the speed with which they complete tasks and the way they manage to meet such short deadlines. They will want a mentor who 'gets on with it', whether that be asking about their family, their hobbies or the task in hand.

Clearly this model is a simplification. In addition, some mentees will have sufficient interpersonal skills to respond reasonably well to any approach. However, the effective mentor will still recognize the importance of choosing a style carefully with most mentees, especially in the early stages of the relationship. With some, therefore, mentors will talk shop a lot; with others they will ask after the mentee's family; with yet others they will show a genuine interest in the mentee's latest 'adventures'; and with the rest they will maintain a somewhat formal relationship and keep emphasizing that they expect the mentee to make the decisions. And with some they will talk quickly while doing any of these!

Notes

1. A good starting point if you are unfamiliar with MBTI is Myers-Briggs, Isabel, *Gifts Differing*, Consulting Psychologists Press Inc., 1980. Also useful is Lawrence, Gordon, *People Types and Tiger Stripes*, Centre for Applications of Psychological Type Inc., 2nd edn, 1982.

    MBTI can be administered only by those who have completed appropriate training. For more information contact the British Association for Psychological Type, Emmaus House, Clifton Hill, Bristol BS8 4PD, UK or Association for Psychological Type, 9140 Ward Parkway, Kansas City, MO 64114–3313, USA.

2. See Hay, Julie, *Transactional Analysis for Trainers*, McGraw-Hill, 1992.

3. See Hay, Julie, *Working it Out at Work*, Sherwood, 1993.

4. My source for this was a workshop run by Taibi Kahler, plus a booklet by him (no ISBN number): *Managing with the Process Communication Model*, Human Development Publications, 1979. He now runs a licensing programme which takes these ideas much further (and has six categories).

Learning and changing

Mentors in traditional schemes are usually selected because they have an appropriate track record—they have succeeded in an area in which the mentee aspires to follow them. Mentors in developmental alliances, on the other hand, will not need such qualities. They are seeking to be guides rather than gurus; their aim is to facilitate growth in the mentee rather than to pass on the lessons from their own experiences. They will therefore need a working knowledge of the processes of learning and changing, and particularly of the levels of learning that are possible.

Levels of learning

Transformational learning is a *deep* level of learning. We can distinguish between three learning levels.

- *Traditional* level learning is about how to do things. This is the sort of learning that is most closely associated with coaching and teaching. What is to be done may already have been defined, so the focus now is on how to do it properly. This may extend into doing different things, as when someone is transferred or promoted to different work.

  This level of learning may occur when the mentor is a subject specialist, such as in traditional apprenticeship programmes or the Civil Service Heads of Profession format described in Chapter 4. Or it may be about change, through events such as organizational restructurings, new technology, or individual advancement.

  Within a developmental alliance, this type of learning may appropriately be tackled as part of an action plan which involves the mentee in seeking out coaches and training courses. The mentor might act as the 'clearing house' if the mentee needs help in pulling together their learning from different 'teachers'.

- *Transitional* level learning is about doing things differently. This format may come closer to a counselling approach, especially if the mentee is finding it hard to change. Like traditional learning, it may be required because of organizationally or individually initiated changes.

  The key here is that learners make transitions and access deeper levels of awareness. They do not simply add some new options to their repertoire—they take out something that was already there and replace it with something else. Hence the connection with counselling; they may need extra help to open up their perspective on the world and make changes to it.

Within a developmental alliance, the mentor may well be able to offer a supportive environment while the mentee comes to terms with the changes, especially if these have been imposed by the organization. However, the mentor will need to guard against becoming too much of a 'wise counsellor', who analyses the problem on behalf of the mentee instead of helping them to move into deeper learning.

■ *Transformational* learning is learning at the deepest level. It is about learning to learn, and is the level a developmental alliance should target. With transformational learning, mentees still change their perspective, but this time they also have an awareness of the process by which they are doing so. They play an equal part in analysing what is happening, so that mentor and mentee work in partnership to increase the mentee's openness to learning.

For example, a mentor within a developmental alliance will expect to share with the mentee the frameworks that follow in the rest of this chapter. The mentor will also be willing to apply alternative models if the mentee prefers. It is impossible to facilitate transformational learning in another person without accepting that we will learn from that person too.

Mentor learning levels

We can see the same levels of learning as they apply in the way a mentor develops.

Traditional learning is about learning the various skills and approaches. At this level the mentors are mostly focused on their own learning, concentrating on doing things right. As with new counsellors, mentors may get locked into using the same technique for everything until they have become skilled enough to let it go.

With transitional learning the focus is shifted to the impact on the mentee. The mentor now has a reasonable degree of skill in using several approaches and is therefore able to choose from a range of options. For example, the mentor may consciously decide when to be supportive, when to be confrontative and so on, and then select which technique to use to achieve the desired result.

Transformational learning for the mentor occurs when they can forget about skills and techniques and pay attention instead to the process taking place between mentor and mentee. Using the conscious/unconscious competence model suggested by Howell[1], the mentor has attained unconscious competence at the transitional learning level and can therefore move deeper.

Learning styles

Having considered the levels of learning, we next borrow from Kolb[2], as developed further by Honey and Mumford[3], to consider the different *ways* in which mentees might learn. Figure 11.1 shows the Learning Cycle (complete with donkey-bridge).

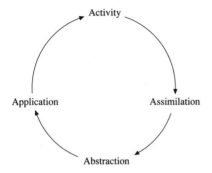

Figure 11.1   *The learning cycle.*

The learning cycle notion suggests that although ideally we need to complete the circle for maximum learning, most of us have a tendency to dwell more in only one or two segments. Thus, we may be restricted in the ways in which we 'accept' learning—and hence mentoring.

- *Activists* learn through *activity*. These are the individuals who just get on and do something. Their learning appears to emerge from the doing, without any conscious attempt to understand or analyse what is happening.
- *Reflectors* learn through *assimilation*. They take time to reflect on what has happened. They like to question others about their experiences, to discuss what has happened or what might happen, to consider a range of points of view.
- *Theorists* learn via *abstraction*. These are the people who pull out the rules and generalizations. In this way they arrive at theories which will guide their future actions. They will also use theories put forward by others provided these stand up to challenge.
- *Pragmatists* are more interested in *application*. They want to know if something will *work*. They like to be given practical suggestions, hints and tips. They also prefer to learn from someone who is already expert at doing the job in question.

There are several ways in which an awareness of learning styles can contribute to the effectiveness of mentoring. It will provide clues about the most effective behaviour for the mentor to use; it will explain why different mentees seem to respond differently to the various stages of the developmental alliance; and it will serve as a guide to selection of development activities. It will also remind mentor and mentee of the need sometimes to focus on the neglected aspects of the cycle, so that the mentoring also becomes a process of learning how to learn.

Activists

Activists will value most a mentor who encourages them to try things out. They need an atmosphere in which mistakes are accepted as a valuable part of learning. The mentor may have to build in appropriate protection by challenging them if they start to take too many risks. They will also benefit from a mentor who insists they take time afterwards to reflect, pull out the lessons and translate these into practical ideas.

Activist mentees may well be the people least likely to come to a mentoring session. They will want to take action, so their first choice will be application and not a session with the mentor at all. However, they may tolerate the action planning stage in order to:

- work out how to create an environment in which they can safely try out their ideas
- have the mentor play devil's advocate to help them select the best options
- break down larger goals into smaller objectives which can be quickly implemented.

The dangers with activists are that they may:

- be too impatient to consider the wisdom of their choices
- make mistakes which could affect their future careers
- experiment with too many options at once
- make no attempt to understand the mentoring process.

Reflectors

Reflectors want time to review. They will appreciate a patient mentor, who accepts their need to check things out thoroughly before taking any action. (These are the learners who read the entire manual before touching the terminal—unlike the activists who play with the keyboard first and only refer to the manual in desperation after they have crashed the system.)

Reflectors are likely to keep learning logs and will be keen to review the process of mentoring. They may need to be pushed to try out new ideas, to experiment with different ways of learning and to accept that a good theory can save many hours of careful consideration of options.

Unlike activists, reflectors will probably be very enthusiastic about mentoring. They will be most comfortable at the assessing stage. They will appreciate:

- talking about themselves and their experiences
- telling the mentor about their mind maps
- answering questions in detail
- having the mentor paraphrase their comments
- any self-disclosure by the mentor.

Their second choice may well be the alternatives stage, when again they will enjoy:

- taking time to review many options
- finding out what others, such as spot mentors, think.

The potential problems when mentoring reflectors will be that:

- they want to spend too much time assessing instead of moving on to analysis
- they consider so many alternatives that they cannot choose between them
- they get overly interested in the experiences of the mentor
- they invite inappropriate self-disclosure from the mentor
- they bring the opinions of their friends to the mentoring sessions.

Theorists

Theorists will want to discuss the theory of mentoring. They will also challenge any assumptions—not to be difficult, but to check that any theory takes account of all possibilities. Their mentor will need the confidence and intellect to engage in what may seem like academic debates. Theorists also like an assurance that any theories are respectable and reputable, with a pedigree of references. They will not accept a mentor's home-grown frameworks.

Theorists may need prompting to pay more attention to practicalities. They may also have to learn to value the general opinions of others, even when these are not presented as theories. They may need encouragement to experiment without first insisting on theorizing.

These mentees will prefer the analysis stage, where they will be happy to:

- use theories to understand their past experiences
- learn new frameworks from the mentor
- teach the mentor the models they know

- apply models such as a SWOT analysis
- identify trends and make patterns with information.

They will also enjoy the process of reviewing the mentoring itself, when they will:

- apply as many models as possible to understanding the interactions between them and the mentor
- be comfortable about giving and receiving feedback based on theoretical frameworks.

Difficulties which may arise are that theorist mentees may:

- suffer from 'paralysis through analysis'
- reject the theories offered by the mentor as not being academically respectable
- use theory as a way of distancing themselves from real contact
- spend too much time reviewing the process
- use the theories to criticize the mentor.

Pragmatists

Pragmatists are focused firmly on whether something will work or not. They are likely to dismiss any mentor who has not also done the job—a difficult requirement to meet in these days of rapid change where a job or task may not actually have existed before. In some ways, pragmatists may be the most difficult people to mentor. They may be so keen to pick up ideas for immediate, practical use that they forget to plan for the future. They will also be the ones most likely to lure the mentor into giving advice.

Mentees who are pragmatists will probably prefer the alternatives stage, when they can:

- concentrate on solutions to problems
- generate plenty of practical ideas
- identify different ways to succeed at work
- find spot mentors to use as role models
- apply their SWOT analysis as a basis for real action.

The risks are that they may:

- disregard a mentor who is not an 'expert' in the work arena
- shun a mentor who admits they are still learning how to be a mentor
- want the mentor to tell them what to do
- lack interest in reviewing the mentoring process
- skip the action planning stage and use only ideas which are easily applicable.

The competence curve

Learning, in whatever style, leads to change. One stage of a developmental alliance is action planning—clearly change is meant to follow. Nowadays, change routinely occurs for many other reasons too, and is not always welcomed. There are ways in which mentors, and mentees themselves, can take steps to make the process of change a more stimulating and less stressful experience than it often turns out to be. One framework for understanding the process is the *competence curve* shown in Figure 11.2.

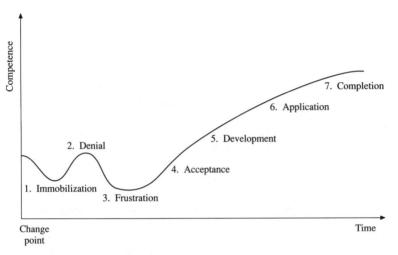

Figure 11.2 *The competence curve.*

This curve contrasts competence with time elapsed since a change occurred. We can see that competence drops initially, appears to rise again, drops yet again and then steadily rises until full competence is attained, sometimes at a higher level than before the change took place.

Phase 1: Immobilization

During Phase 1 competence drops suddenly. A mentee may appear to be in a state of suspended animation, marking time, not doing anything. This is a necessary stage in development, and is part of the normal process of dealing with change. It is similar to the hiatus that occurs when we reach the 'mid-life crisis' (although hopefully not lasting as long!).

A mentee may seem to be immobilized for a while, even when the change was one they actually initiated. With an imposed change, such as redundancy, their reaction might even be labelled 'shock'. Mentees need time to absorb the change and to compare their old expectations to the new reality.

Mentees probably lack information about the new situation so do not know what to do. They may be afraid of doing it wrong and appearing stupid, so that fear of the unknown shows up as paralysis. Or perhaps they simply lack the motivation to make the change work. Even with a change that was chosen and planned, a psychologically healthy person needs a short period in which to simply experience being in a new situation before they are expected to take action.

Phase 2: Denial

Phase 2 involves denial. Mentees may act as if behaviour patterns from the past will still be appropriate. Again, even if they have chosen the transition, they may hope that their existing skills and knowledge will still be enough. Some of these skills will probably be useful, but severe problems due to denial may arise because mentees fear failure, and rationalize that what worked for them in the past should still work now. Perhaps they feel a threat to their level of competence and skill, making them reluctant to experiment with new behaviours. Or they may be simply custom-bound or in a rut.

Strangely, they may actually appear to be performing better during this phase than in Phase 1. This is because they now start applying their skills and knowledge and are therefore seen to be achieving things. Unfortunately, they will not be using behaviour that relates to the current job, and this will gradually become evident. People will start to question the mentees' grasp of reality, or think that they are being deliberately obtuse. The mentees, on the other hand, are unaware of their denial and continue to behave in the way that was successful previously. Slowly, they allow their defence systems to weaken, and start to notice the need for change.

Phase 3: Frustration

In Phase 3 mentees go through a period of frustration. They now recognize that they need to behave differently, but they don't know how. Their frustration arises because they feel incompetent during their efforts to apply new approaches. Indeed, others too may perceive them as incompetent as they struggle with new skills, new knowledge, new situations—and this means that they become even more conscious of their shortcomings. In some cases, mentees turn their frustration against others and seek to blame them for their position. Even when they chose the change, they can blame others for not helping them enough, not training them properly beforehand. They may even blame the mentor for not warning them against the problems they now face.

Feeding into their frustration will be the potential overload due to their genuine need to learn new approaches. Mentees may also fear a loss of status through decreased competence and the loss of their power base or their network of contacts.

So in Phase 3 mentees struggle to work out how they should be different, what new skills they need and what qualities are required in the new situation. They are likely to need to do a great deal of thinking about this.

Phase 4: Acceptance

At Phase 4 mentees move into acceptance, and let go of the attitudes and behaviours that were comfortable and useful in the past. They now have the answers from Phase 3 and can begin the process of acquiring new patterns. They start to test out new ways of doing things. There will still be occasional moments of frustration, however, such as when their new skills are not quite practised enough or they identify yet another area where they lack knowledge.

This phase represents the move, psychologically, into the mentee's personal learning cycle. Mentees recognize the reality of their experience— that they are in a new situation and need a new set of behaviours. They review the situation and compare it with the past to identify differences. They analyse the differences and develop frameworks for understanding where they are now. Then they begin to actively experiment.

During Phase 4 mentees may still appear incompetent to a degree. They are working out their identity in the changed situation so, although they have now accepted the change, there will still be temporary problems as they try out new approaches.

Phase 5: Development

All being well, mentees will move on to Phase 5: development. In this phase, they concentrate on developing the skills and knowledge required in the new situation, and become increasingly competent at operating in the changed environment. They make decisions about the most effective techniques and then become skilled in using them. Their knowledge increases, so that others come to regard them as the appropriate experts in their field.

It is worth noting that organizations often attempt to rush this stage. They provide training as soon as the person has changed to a new role, and much of the impact is lost. This is because individuals cannot relate the training provision to the needs of the new job until they have clarified their new identity. They cannot clarify their identity without having time to think; they cannot think until they have explored; they do not feel safe to explore until they have come to terms with the change.

Phase 6: Application

In Phase 6 mentees move on to application. Most importantly, they now consolidate their identity in their changed role. They develop their own views on how the job should be done, how they should relate to others and how others should relate to them. They resolve in their own minds the questions about their status, their beliefs about the situation and their view of the organization. In particular, they work out how they fit into the new scheme of things.

Phase 7: Completion

Entering Phase 7 means that completion has been achieved. Mentees now feel comfortable and competent once again—so much so that they are no longer conscious of having experienced a transition. They are really into the new situation and have ceased to compare it, favourably or unfavourably, with their position before the change.

The phases of competence		
Stage	Competence	Behaviour
1. Immobilization	drops	We seem to do nothing, to withdraw or mark time
2. Denial	appears to rise	We act as if nothing has changed and go on as we used to
3. Frustration	drops again	We know we need to change but don't know how
4. Acceptance	begins to rise	We start exploring options that might be appropriate to the new situation
5. Development	continues to rise	We develop our new skills and knowledge so as to become competent performers
6. Application	is consolidated	We apply our new skills within our new situation
7. Completion	maximum competence is evident	We are through the transition and are no longer conscious of having been through a change

The cycle of change

There will be many times during the course of a mentoring relationship when change will occur for a mentee. Indeed, the point of the mentoring is to enable the mentee to identify what it is they want to change (and then how to go about changing it). The competence curve provides a framework so that mentors can better judge how to provide appropriate support and challenge—the style of this will vary over the cycle of the change.

During *Phase 1* the mentee needs reassurance. They need to know that the mentor will not desert them because they are not doing anything. It can be very helpful to be reminded that this is a normal human response to change and that it will not last forever. The quality of the human bond will be critical here, with a high premium on rapport, empathy and having a clear contract which specifically includes using the mentoring relationship as a form of mentee support.

During *Phase 2* the mentor will have to demonstrate much patience. It will be tempting to challenge the mentee about their denial—but full-frontal attacks rarely succeed in getting someone to recognize their unconscious discounting. It is a case of 'We don't know what we don't know'. Questioning may help, as might summarizing, to nudge the mentee into recognizing some of the inconsistencies.

During this phase the mentee really needs to explore. The mentor can help best by prompting them to do that—to check out new circumstances, to initiate meetings with new colleagues, to find a personal way around the new situation. This will give the mentee the necessary data to complete the next phase of the change process. Meetings with spot mentors may also be appropriate, to gather information and ask them about options.

The frustration during *Phase 3* often arises because the mentee is now thinking about the new circumstances. The mentor will need to exhibit tolerance, especially if they have strong opinions about the situation. The mentee does not want to be told what to do—they want to work it out for themselves. Mentors can also be helpful by pointing out to the mentee that managers, and others, may find it hard to be tolerant, so the mentee may be wise to monitor what they say in the workplace. Expressing too many personal opinions about the faults of the previous regime may make the mentee somewhat unpopular, and showing anger and frustration is likely to lead to even worse problems.

In *Phase 4* the mentee is at last coming to terms with the change. Now they need support from the mentor for making decisions alone. During this phase the mentee will be deciding on their 'new identity'—who they are going to be now that a change has occurred. For example, they may determine what sort of professional person they will be—perhaps knowledgeable about specific aspects of the work, or especially good at presenting ideas, or the person who will save the section .... It will be important that the mentor does not interject personal opinions here; the decision on identity must be owned by the mentee.

It is not until a person has reworked personal identity and accepted the change that they are ready to learn how to be such a person. In *Phase 5*, therefore, the mentee wants to acquire the extra skills and knowledge that they need to perform effectively. The role of the mentor at this stage will be to help the mentee consider options, make plans and take action to secure the appropriate training and coaching. Spot mentoring may again be useful to help the mentee clarify what might be needed. The mentor can also help by encouraging the mentee to consider a broad range of training approaches so that they think of more than formal training courses.

In *Phase 6*, when the mentee begins to apply new learning, the mentor can reinforce this by discussing its applicability with them. They can help the mentee to consider how best to use the ideas they are acquiring during training sessions, how to gain as much as possible from any coaching, how to get maximum benefit from open learning and how to observe others and copy what they see (or do it differently).

Finally, at *Phase 7* the change is completed. The mentor can now help the mentee to celebrate success. They can also review together the way in which the mentee has dealt with the change, pulling out any lessons for the future. If the change process has been a major one, such as a job change, this may also be the time at which the mentee is ready to move on to another mentor. In that case, the celebration can also include mutual recognition of the benefits gained from the relationship.

We can link the stages of the competence curve with the stages of the developmental alliance as follows:

- *Immobilization*: need for reassurance, contact
- *Alliance*: emphasis on bonding and that the mentor/mentee contract is firmly in place

- *Denial*: need patience, gentle challenge
- *Assessment*: begin to explore the facts of the situation

- *Frustration*: need tolerance, chance to share their thinking
- *Analysis*: help them identify patterns and trends

- *Acceptance*: need reinforcement of their right and ability to decide for themselves
- *Alternatives*: make sure they consider a wide enough range of options

- *Development*: need encouragement to get appropriate training and coaching
- *Action planning*: stimulation to consider a variety of training and development options

- *Application*: need the chance to work out how to apply their learning to best effect
- *Application*: support while they use their new learning and work out what else might be needed

- *Completion*: need to celebrate their success at completing the change
- *Appraisal*: opportunity to review the overall process of change and satisfy themselves that they have moved in the direction chosen.

The spirals of development

This model of competence and change is based on a theory of child development[4]. In this framework, we are shown that the stages actually occur repeatedly throughout life. We all complete the first six phases by the time we are about 19 years old; the seventh stage represents the fact that we continue to start new cycles at regular intervals. Our timings may vary individually, but often seem to match a 13- or 19-year pattern. People may well decide that they want mentoring at the time that they are starting a new cycle biologically.

We can imagine this as a spiralling effect, with one major life cycle and a series of smaller cycles each time changes occur. Rather like a set of Russian dolls, there are ever smaller cycles contained within larger ones. For instance, we may be halfway through a major life cycle when we enter a new relationship. A smaller, but still fairly lengthy, cycle may begin. Then, within that, we may change employer. Again, a somewhat smaller cycle starts up. Perhaps we may now change jobs within the same organization, leading to a still smaller cycle. And so on and so on ....

It is difficult to be precise about the length of such spirals as this will be influenced by many factors. For instance, how responsive is the person to change—do they enjoy it and see it as a challenge or hate it and fight it all the way? How extensive is the impact of the change—does it affect the person's whole way of life or is it restricted to work, social life, family life, etc? How supportive an environment is the person in—do friends, colleagues, family show extra care or is the individual expected to cope alone?

Allowing for these individual differences, we can say that a 'typical' job change for a professional is likely to take two or three years. It is interesting to note that many organizations are now reorganizing so frequently that employees may not have time to complete a spiral before the next change is imposed. High stress levels arise when people who have barely passed through the frustration stage are suddenly pitchforked back into a new situation. Rather like snakes and ladders, they have to go back and start again. This means that they miss out on the opportunity to experience themselves as competent—it should not be a surprise that this results in increased levels of frustration as they cycle round again.

A mentoring relationship will start its own spiral—for both mentor and mentee! Depending on the individuals involved, this may well last up to two years. It is sensible, therefore, for mentor and mentee to anticipate that they will be together for about that long and agree their contract accordingly.

Being aware of this also helps with the ending of the relationship. It will come naturally when the mentee feels that the spiral has been completed. Before then, there will be a period of consolidation during the application phase; as mentor and mentee become aware of this, they know that it will soon be time to move on. This will avoid the problem of the 'everlasting mentor' who never lets go, or the 'perpetual mentee' who continues to cling.

Helping strategies

There are a variety of ways in which we can help other people. We might tell them what to do, gently suggest what to do, ask them what they propose to do—each of these options will help them, but in a different way. One of the key skills in mentoring is choosing the most appropriate helping strategy. One of the ways in which we can make that choice easier is by having a framework for classifying different strategies, along with information about the potential advantages and disadvantages of each method.

We can do this quite straightforwardly by considering how much 'work' each person does on the 'task'. By 'work', I mean directly addressing the task rather than applying skills to help the other person do this. By 'task', I mean whatever the content of the session is about. For example, the task might be to work out how to improve the mentee's time management; 'work' in that case would be coming up with ideas about how to manage time, suggesting ways to implement these ideas, and so on. When a mentor offers information and advice about time management, they are doing part of the 'work'. When the mentor uses questions to get the mentee talking about time management, then the mentee is doing the 'work'.

Figure 11.3 shows a simple classification system for this. At one extreme, the mentor does all the work; taking over the task and dealing with it single-handed. At the other end of the scale, the mentor does nothing and leaves it to the mentee to handle. Between these limits, there are several options. Teaching the mentee something still means that the mentor is

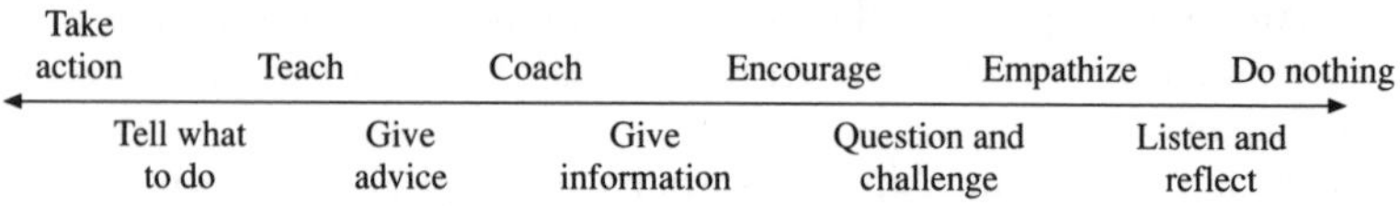

Take action	Teach	Coach	Encourage	Empathize	Do nothing
Tell what to do	Give advice	Give information	Question and challenge	Listen and reflect	

Figure 11.3 *The helping continuum.*

working a lot on the task, while at the same time the mentee does some work on relating the teaching to personal circumstances. Giving advice still has the mentor working on the task, but now the mentee has to work hard too, as it will be up to them to decide whether to accept the advice. Encouraging is probably the counterbalance to advising; now the major part of the work is done by the mentee in coming up with a proposed course of action. The work for the mentor, in this case, consists of deciding whether the mentee's suggestion should be given encouragement—will it meet the needs of the task? And then there is listening, where the mentee is doing nearly all of the work while the mentor's direct involvement with the task is limited to paying attention to what the mentee says about it.

The choice of helping strategy will be affected, appropriately or inappropriately, by several things:

- The *perceived* roles of the mentor and the mentee. Our perceptions are powerful influences on our behaviour—if we see things in a certain way we act accordingly. Therefore, if we perceive ourselves to be in a traditional mode of mentoring, we will tend to operate closer to the left-hand end of the scale because we expect the mentor to know best. The more we see our arrangement as a developmental alliance, the further we will move towards the right.
- The *actual* roles of the mentor and the mentee. If the mentor is more senior than the mentee, there will be a temptation to move towards the right because we expect the mentor to take greater responsibility for the outcome. We also know that the mentor has more authority, so there is a tendency for mentees to 'do as they are told'.
- Age will also be a factor. Even though logically we may know that an older mentor is not necessarily wiser than a younger mentee, we will still have a natural human inclination to let the older person take the lead. It is easier to shift towards the right if we are the same age. If the mentor is younger than the mentee, we may even have an unconscious struggle to find a helping style that feels right.
- Our gender may well be significant. Although there are always exceptions, most men communicate in a different way from most women. Men are more likely to focus on telling someone how easily they will be able to resolve an issue, so may tend to shift to the left. Women, on the other hand, are more prone to empathizing and demonstrating that they have had similar issues to deal with, so will end up at the right-hand end of the strategy scale.
- The personal styles of the mentor and the mentee. Watch people for only a short time and you will soon see that many of us show the same characteristics over and over again. We can sort people into five broad groups: the controllers, the nurturers, the computers, the adaptors and

the spontaneous. Mentors with high controller tendencies will opt for helping strategies to the left of the scale. Nurturers will operate somewhat left and middle, from advising through to encouraging. Computer mentors will ask questions and engage in joint problem solving, so they are most likely to function at the right-hand end. Adaptors may struggle to be mentors because they expect the mentee to tell them what to do. Spontaneous mentors will be open about their own feelings, so they may also be effective at empathizing and counselling, provided they don't hijack the session to deal with their own issues.

The personal style of the mentee will also be important. Controller mentees will object to being told what to do; nurturer mentees will want to take care of the mentor; computer mentees will want their mentor to move between the strategies depending on the immediate needs of the mentee; adaptor mentees will subtly set the mentor up to do the work for them; and spontaneous mentees may actually need a controller or nurturer to keep them focused on the task.

■ Our thinking styles. We also differ in the ways in which we think and reach conclusions. Some of us want to gather the facts, weigh up the possibilities and come to a conclusion. Others rely far more on 'gut feeling' and intuition. Yet others pay most attention to the ways people have previously dealt with similar tasks.

If we are 'logical' thinkers, we will prefer our mentors to use questioning, listening and reflecting skills to help us check that we have covered all options. A preference for intuition will mean that we want our mentor to encourage us, but not to expect us to explain our reasons (although, if we're wise, we'll also want them to challenge us a bit). If we are more interested in what other people have done, we will look to our mentor to provide us with this sort of information and to give us the benefit of their own experiences.

As mentor, we are likely to adopt whichever helping strategy best fits our own thinking style. If we and the mentee share a style, we may then feel very comfortable with each other, but run the risk of overlooking things. If our styles clash, we may decide we have a 'personality problem', or we may recognize that the mentee will make better decisions if we make the most of our different thinking styles.

■ The characteristic working styles of mentor and mentee must also be taken into account. Again, we can roughly sort working styles into categories: doing things fast; doing them perfectly; doing them so that others are pleased; doing them enthusiastically; or doing them calmly. As with our thinking styles, matching working styles may feel good, but lead to oversights, while conflicting working styles may lead to tension, but may also improve our joint results. Perfectly or pleasing others may shift us towards having the mentor tell the mentee what to do. Fast or enthusiastically may incline us to the right; we either have no time to listen to the mentor or we already have many ideas of our own. Calmly will probably operate comfortably across the range, with the result being more important than how we got there.

■ Our learning styles should be an important factor. Do we learn best through practical experience, through trying something out, through thinking over and reviewing what has happened, or through developing some generalizations so that we know what to do next time? There is a risk that mentors assume their mentees have the same approach to learning as they do. Often this will not be the case. The first two styles mean that most of our learning may well take place away from the mentoring discussion, so we need a mentor who will help us work out how to set up appropriate situations for ourselves (or perhaps to set them up for us—right-hand end!). The last two indicate a need for questioning, listening and maybe some information.

■ Previous experiences usually have a big effect on how we behave. If we have been a mentor or a mentee before, we are likely to expect to continue with whatever strategies were used in the past—perhaps without even stopping to think about whether they are still relevant. If we have not been in a mentoring relationship before, we may still continue with an expectation based on what other people have told us about their mentoring.

■ History! It may seem strange, but we all carry with us all sorts of psychological baggage from the past. Unwittingly, we are influenced in the present by forgotten events which happened many years before. The way our parents brought us up, the way our teachers treated us, the way our early managers and supervisors related to us, will all have fashioned what we do now. If we have been used to authority figures, we'll expect the same from the mentor. If we were brought up to take plenty of initiative, we'll expect to do so as a mentee. As mentor, we will reproduce the parent or supervisory figures that we once knew and have forgotten.

Notes

1. Howell, W . S., *The Empathic Communicator*, Wadsworth, 1982.
2. Kolb, D. A., *Experiential Learning*, Prentice-Hall, 1984.
3. Honey, Peter and Mumford, Alan, *The Manual of Learning Styles*, Peter Honey, 1986. This manual includes a copy of the Learning Styles Questionnaire. For details, contact Peter Honey at 10 Linden Avenue, Maidenhead, Berks SL6 6HB, UK.
4. Levin, Pamela, *Becoming the Way We Are*, 3rd edn, and *Cycles of Power: A*

User's Guide to the Seven Seasons of Life both published by Health Communications Inc., 1988.

For a more detailed explanation of how the various stages in childhood are precursors to the Competence Curve, see Hay, Julie, *Working it Out at Work*, Sherwood, 1993.

Initiating a corporate approach

CHAPTER

12

There are several ways in which developmental alliances might be introduced:

- as a corporate initiative which reinforces a change in culture, such as towards a learning organization
- as a means of stimulating a culture change towards greater equality
- by mentors in existing, more traditional schemes, as a way of moving towards a more 'democratic' style of mentoring
- by individuals with traditional mentors, to invite those mentors to move to a different style
- by individuals who want the benefits of being mentored but lack access to a corporate scheme.

There is something paradoxical about introducing developmental alliances as a corporate initiative—how can we 'organize' such an approach when it relies so much on individuals taking responsibility for their own development? We are likely to need an approach resembling that of an Employee Assistance Programme, preferably one staffed by volunteers rather than professionals. This will mean that 'the organization' makes the time and training available, encourages people to become mentors, indicates that there is a commitment to having employees use the service, and makes no attempt to coerce people. It will be important to make sure that managers share the commitment, so that they do not put obstacles in the way of employees wanting time for mentoring.

Checking the paradigm

A key element in such an approach will be the paradigm that exists within people's minds. The metaphors described in Chapter 2 may not be suitable. Thinking about our organization as a machine or as a political system carries with it a sense of predictability and inflexibility, with change occurring only when the machine or system breaks down. Brains and cultures conjure up an image in which things happen without us truly understanding the process. Psychic prisons and instruments of domination are hardly likely to welcome an approach that advocates greater freedom for individuals to grow. Even the spider plant is a problem—the plantlets are either dependent on the big pot for nourishment, or they put down their own roots and break off contact with the centre as well as with each other.

The flux, transformation, flowing river type of images are perhaps the most useful. They do at least capture the essence of constant change and movement. However, these may also be potentially deficient because they concentrate on what the organization *is* rather than what it *could be*.

We really need a paradigm which allows a vision of the future to be created. It is as if we need a paradigm of a paradigm, that will enable us to recognize that we are playing with mental models, and that organizations are more complex than our limited understanding of them. We need a way of envisioning a future metaphor as well as one that represents the present.

We also need an image that comes close to a learning organization, or a community. The nature of the community will be significant—preferably not the sort of quasi-religious community in which the followers give up all their possessions or blindly follow the leader! Instead, it needs to include individuals coming together with an aim of supporting and challenging each other as they grow and develop themselves.

This kind of thinking encompasses the other key element—that the paradigm consists of what the organization *is* rather than what it *does*. Our vision of the future should be of how the organization will be, seen from inside and outside. Perhaps the image of a constellation would be appropriate, with the notion that the perception changes depending on which planet you occupy. Thus, there will be a climate for each area and each planet, there will be the gravitational pushes and pulls between them, the ways in which movement of one planet causes the tide to rise on another, and so on.

This image captures the underlying, yet constant, movement that goes on. It also reminds us that much damage is done to the environment if we fail to consider the long-term consequences of our actions; that we pollute other areas if we behave selfishly; that we destroy other species if we think only of our own needs. (It also allows us to view certain market forces as if they were meteors which we could not have forecast without much better scanning equipment than we have now—and highlights the need to develop better 'telescopes'.)

Checking the pathology

Another option for assessing the condition of an organization is to look specifically for signs of pathology. What else do we need to take into account if we opt for transformational mentoring? Why do initiatives like this fail? Why is it sometimes so difficult to introduce new approaches, even when we all seem to agree that they are needed? There is so much that has been written about organizations and about individual growth that it seems inconceivable that anything remains to be said. Yet, in spite of all that has been produced, organizations and individuals continue to search for new ways to grow and develop and then fail to implement them effectively.

So what happens? Are we reinventing the wheel, are we changing so fast that new ideas are constantly needed, or are we sabotaging ourselves in some way? I suspect the latter.

It is more than a decade since Manfred Kets de Vries and Danny Miller wrote *The Neurotic Organization*[1], in which they pointed out that covert psychological processes operating in organizations were usually ignored by management theorists. They suggested that a concentration on neurotic behaviour would provide the basis for a taxonomy of organizational dysfunctioning.

More recently, Gerard Egan[2] has borrowed the Jungian concept of the *shadow side* to refer to the hidden agendas and covert operations which most of us recognize as a mix of office politics and psychopathology— and which transactional analysts call psychological games. Egan exhorts us to clean up the shadow side because it makes sound economic sense. Oppressive managers, self-serving deals between departments, appraisal schemes that are a farce and unhealthy organizational norms, all drive up costs.

It is not difficult to relate these ideas to the trends now affecting organizations and individuals. The current interest in organizational transformation mirrors the trend for individuals to place more emphasis on quality of life. As individuals start cashing out and cocooning themselves, so they will reject organizations that expect them to fit the old, psychologically unhealthy patterns.

Addictive organizations

Schaef and Fassel[3] describe an addictive organization in ways which sound worryingly familiar!

First, they point out that an addictive system is a closed system—it calls for addictive behaviours. By this, they mean that there are no options. People are not allowed to think for themselves, but are expected to conform to norms that may well be unspoken but are extremely powerful.

Some of the major characteristics of such an organization are:

- *Denial*: We are convinced that we are not addicted, we are not overworking, our sales are not really falling

- *Confusion*: We are not sure what is going on, but we thrive on chaos
- *Self-centredness*: Everything that happens is deliberately directed at us, either as an affirmation or an attack
- *Dishonesty*: We don't talk about it, we are expected to cheat, we pretend we know what is going on, we even stay out of touch with our own feelings
- *Perfectionism*: We are obsessed with not being good enough, we quickly cover up mistakes instead of learning from them
- *Scarcity model*: There is never enough time, money, attention ...
- *Illusion of control*: We are constantly trying to control—ourselves, other people, the system
- *Frozen feelings*: Feelings are signs of weakness; we stay out of touch with them in case we can't handle it
- *Ethical deterioration*: The addictive system invites us to compromise our spirit
- *Dependency*: If we can get someone else to take the decisions, then we don't have to accept any responsibility.

This is not the complete list! There will also be stress, depression, defensiveness, negativism, forgetfulness, projection, tunnel vision, fear—and probably more.

The addiction hologram

The organization will be a replica of the addictive individuals within it—imagine the cauliflower that I mentioned earlier as the image for a hologram. At each level the same processes will be acted out. This means that we have:

- *The key person as addict*: For example, the senior manager who is a workaholic and puts pressure on everyone else to be the same
- *The individual as addict*: The person who is 'powerless' to resist the addictive nature of the organizational culture, or who brings to it personal pre-existing hang-ups
- *The co-dependent as addict*: The person who is addicted to taking care of the 'overt' addict, who works just as hard at this and is at a loss if the addict recovers
- *The organization as addictive substance*: For the people who are totally addicted to work, who live for the job, who see the organization as a substitute family
- *The organization as addict*: The companies which behave just like addicts, which have secrets and gossip, suffer from corporate forgetfulness and blame the outside world for problems that are really internal

■ *The organization as co-dependent*: Like individuals, these operate
with the same patterns as addicts, including the belief that someone
else has the problem–so they set out to save the dysfunctional
organizations from themselves and fail.

These levels of addiction are maintained via a number of underlying
processes. One key is the promise of future reward; this means that we
ignore what is happening to us now because we expect it to lead to
something so much better. So we overwork, for example, with the
expectation that this will earn us promotion, or security, or recognition.
Or an addictive organization compulsively restructures in the belief that
this will lead to future profits.

Other processes relate to maintenance of the psychic equilibrium. This
involves absorbing any differences or redefining into insignificance
anything that cannot be tolerated. If someone within an addictive
organization starts to rock the boat, they will either be emasculated by
being taken over or they will be reframed into something that the system
can deal with.

For instance, an HR professional who points out the true nature of an
addictive organization may be turned into an example of how open to
criticism the organization is (while the content of that criticism is
ignored), or they may be invalidated by claims that they have the facts
wrong or are insufficiently qualified to judge, or they may be accused of
engaging in personality conflicts.

The processes of judgement and decision making will also be suspect.
Addictive organizations will tend towards dualism—decisions will be
treated as choices between two extremes. Both extremes are likely to be
unacceptable, at which point the organization will instead rely on the
perceptions of others to define itself. Ultimate success or failure will
depend on whether outsiders are satisfied, and the organization will lose
the ability to recognize its own identity.

I think that most of us can identify a number of organizations where
we can see addictive patterns at work. This will mean that these
institutions will have some employees who are also addicted, whether it
be to alcohol, work, stress, crises, excitement or long hours.

Transformational mentoring implies a concern with the whole
person—not simply jobs or careers. A developmental alliance may
therefore involve helping the mentee to deal with issues of addiction. I
am not, however, suggesting that a mentor should attempt to deal with a
mentee's drug addiction or alcoholism, although it will certainly be
helpful to know about the subject if an individual asks for support while
seeking active help elsewhere.

There are plenty of other forms of addiction a mentor can help with;
workaholics, for instance, may have lost the ability to enjoy a balanced

lifestyle. Or a mentee may be suffering under the influence of an addictive manager and need to identify healthy options for dealing with this. Remember that mentors may also be addicts—and may then unwittingly pass on the problem to their mentees. Greater awareness of the nature of addictive organizations will help in many ways!

Checking the culture

Having checked the paradigm and the pathology, we next need to assess the culture. Paradigm is a global (or galactic) concept. Culture is more specific; for instance, each part of the constellation will have its own culture. I am using the term 'culture' here to refer to the characteristic or current qualities of the organization in relation to strategies, structures, strokes and stimulation. Some of the aspects to be considered when 'assessing' an organization for its readiness to introduce transformational mentoring are as follows.

Strategies

■ Does the strategy (or mission or vision) of the organization specifically include an expectation of change and personal growth?
■ Is strategy formulated in a participative way—is the vision known and shared?
■ Is there a learning approach to strategy—are people constantly scanning for new data and using these to improve the ways in which they plan?

Structure

■ Are structures designed to allow maximum initiative?
■ Do the structures encourage team working and peer support?
■ Can people move across departmental or functional boundaries easily?
■ Are there self-managing teams and distributed leadership?

Strokes

■ Are people rewarded for initiative and risk-taking
■ Are people recognized for putting effort into developing themselves?
■ Are people encouraged to learn things not directly relevant to their current jobs, or even to the organization?
■ Are people rewarded for helping to develop others—colleagues as well as junior staff?

Stimulation

- Is the atmosphere challenging and exciting?
- Is there a general sense of learning and developing?
- Can ideas be introduced and championed by anyone, regardless of grade or level?
- Is the organization open to new ideas from outside?

Success factors

- Have there been successful corporate initiatives before?
- Have there been occasions when cross-functional groups have been successful?
- Are the existing developmental processes working effectively?
- Are you satisfied that transformational mentoring will contribute to the future success of the organization?

Another simple way of thinking about the culture within an organization is to consider which of the triangles in Figure 12.1 best represents the image that people have.

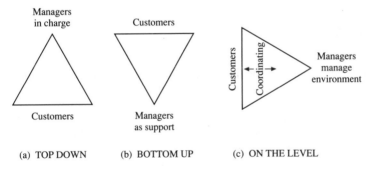

(a) TOP DOWN   (b) BOTTOM UP   (c) ON THE LEVEL

Figure 12.1 *Organizational triangles.*

The *top down* organization has the familiar pyramid shape to denote a hierarchy. Decisions are made at the top and conveyed to the ranks via middle managers. Traditional mentoring will be the preferred option here, with high flyers being groomed to succeed as clones of the existing managers.

In a *bottom up* organization, someone has pointed out that customers are kings and queens. They have therefore reversed the pyramid, to make the point that managers are there to provide the resources that enable front-line workers to do their job of keeping the customer happy.

This change in perspective may well have been accompanied by reductions in the number of managers, so mentoring may have disappeared because the remaining managers are so demoralized or unsure of their own value and the front-line employees are too busy or too stir-crazy to care.

When the organization reaches the *on the level* version, people have recognized that all jobs are equally important. The customer contact jobs are valued, but so is the role of management in dealing with outside bodies such as government departments and local authorities, the City and the shareholders, the local and perhaps the international community. There is even a recognition of the worth of people in between as coordinators and bridges.

In an organization like this, the concept of developmental alliances between equals does not seem strange. There are also likely to be partnerships with suppliers and purchasers, so that developmental alliances across these boundaries also become feasible. This is the type of organization that is most ready for transformational mentoring—although not, of course, the one that needs it the most!

Making it happen

Getting agreement

Assuming your responses to the paradigm, pathology and culture checks are reasonably positive, the first step towards initiating transformational mentoring will be getting agreement from other people within the organization. Again, this is paradoxical, but it is also advisable and professional, especially if you do not have secret yearnings to be a fifth columnist. It may seem tempting to think that you could change the corporate culture with a single-handed initiative; however, this would be incongruent with an approach that is about people working together. It would also increase the likelihood of resistance once your plans become public.

Although many organizations continue to run training programmes and similar activities as an act of faith, it is becoming increasingly necessary to demonstrate a 'bottom-line' impact for this type of human resource undertaking. A key element for organizational acceptance of such approaches nowadays is the expected impact on productivity.

With such a new proposition, we cannot yet quote success stories from elsewhere. However, we can refer to research which shows the benefits of greater employee involvement. Practices designed to generate commitment and flexibility among staff have been shown to link with higher productivity (Guest).[4] In addition, despite much negative comment about their methods of analysis, David Metcalfe and Sue Fernie[5] of the London

School of Economics have provided data showing a strong correlation between productivity and employee involvement, single status and merit pay.

Agreement at a senior level (or generally if you already work in a flat, team-structured organization) is needed for various aspects. The most obvious requirements will be for resources (time, materials, locations) for the introduction of the approach. Examples here are publicity for the scheme, calls for participants, briefing sessions and supporting documentation, mentor and mentee training and familiarization, and ongoing monitoring and evaluation of the project.

Equally important will be agreement to the time to be spent by mentors and mentees, *at any level*, on an ongoing basis. There needs to be recognition and acceptance that transformational mentoring is available to everyone in the organization and not just the perceived high flyers. It is particularly important that this view is communicated, so that managers and supervisors do not start to 'vet' who is allowed to become a mentee or a mentor.

The most significant aspect that needs to be cleared is the focus on individual growth even when that does *not* coincide with the requirements of the organization. Like development centre participants, mentees are likely to gain a clearer awareness of their own strengths—and may well decide that their future lies elsewhere. It will help if there has been specific assent to this potential result of this style of mentoring, so that the scheme is not terminated if valued employees start resigning.

Getting started

As I have already said, the nature of transformational mentoring requires that individuals opt into the process rather than 'obeying' a call from management (or personnel). The start point, therefore, needs to be some method of letting people know that the option exists.

The two obvious ways of doing this are:

- to publicize a potential scheme in a general way and see who expresses interest
- to approach selected individuals who have a reputation for interest in new ideas.

The first option comes closest to the Employee Assistance type of route. It will involve elements such as:

- announcing the initiative in corporate newsletters, via notice boards, as a cascade through meetings
- including details in personnel procedure handbooks or similar manuals that employees consult
- running open briefings to explain the initiative–if appropriate, at

different times and locations so that they are accessible to all (e.g. inside and outside working hours, so that those who do not want to ask their managers for time off to attend can still come along outside normal working hours, during the lunch break, etc.).

The second alternative is more circumspect, but may be more effective in many organizations. It involves identifying those people who are most likely to support the initiative in a practical way. Routes for accessing these people include:

■ Check previous corporate initiatives—who was involved, who was most enthusiastic?
■ Who already makes maximum use of development activities—for example, who attends training courses or sends their staff on them, who uses educational sponsorship provisions or encourages their staff to do so?
■ Who has a reputation for developing others—who, for instance, completes appraisals without being nagged by the personnel department, who volunteers to provide inputs into training courses?
■ Who has an effective network—who seems to know people in many different functions, who manages to organize secondments or temporary assignments for themselves or their staff?
■ Who is very busy–is this because they are enthusiastic about new initiatives?

Having identified your 'prospects', you will need to provide briefings before starting the process of matching mentors and mentees. The core content of these will be the same as if you had opted for a general launch.

Briefings

You may be running these for all comers or you may invite your few hand-picked individuals only. Whichever it is, you will need to cover the following aspects:

■ Why the approach you are about to describe will be of benefit to them and to the organization—for this you will need to have a reasonably good idea about what matters to them, what 'turns them on'
■ What developmental alliances are—a definition and description of how they work, the stages, the skills needed, etc.
■ The situation within the organization—what agreement there is from senior management, what resources will be made available, the level of acceptance regarding time to be spent on mentoring by mentors and mentees
■ What support will be provided—e.g. skills training, help in matching

mentors and mentees, ongoing support available, perhaps facilitation of separate mentor and mentee support groups
- What happens next–how you propose to proceed. For instance, will you operate a 'dating agency' for them or should they now find their own matches? Have you designed a proforma for them so that they can circulate their details, etc?

The nebulous nature of much mentoring means that it can be a difficult concept to grasp. It is therefore likely to be helpful if participants at briefings can be encouraged to 'try it out'. Short sessions in pairs (or triads, with observer) can be invaluable for demonstrating the essence of the developmental alliance approach.

Matchmaking

Having completed the briefings, you will hopefully have a number of volunteer mentors and mentees who will need pairing up in some way. In Chapters 9 and 10 I mentioned a number of characteristics that might be relevant and suggested some frameworks for assessing people. You may have other qualities which you think are significant, or other models which you prefer to use.

Whatever you choose, you will need a procedure for the matching process. Again, there are several options:

- Being a matchmaking agency: collecting data on mentors and mentees, comparing and contrasting and then allocating people into pairs, who may meet by themselves or with a facilitator present initially
- Being a dating agency: collecting information and making this available, anonymously if necessary, to prospective mentors and mentees, who then arrange to follow up directly with those who look promising
- Being an independent adviser: collecting data, analysing them, and giving prospective mentors/mentees information on a small number of people who might be best fits, then helping them to make a choice
- Being a party host/hostess: organizing a gathering of mentors and mentees, with 'getting-to-know-you' activities, so that they can mingle and make their own choices
- Encouraging a do-it-yourself approach: suggesting that mentors and mentees make their own arrangements, such as through networking.

For the latter, an idea adapted from the growing world of multi-level marketing (MLM) may be helpful to mentees. To create a large network, new MLM distributors are advised to *make a list*. On this list they put the names of *everyone* they know. There is no sifting at this stage: they are encouraged to think of friends, relatives, colleagues, acquaintances and people they do business with. Within these categories they are also prompted to recall colleagues from past jobs, contacts made through voluntary associations, parents of children's friends, people they buy from, people met at church, social clubs, sports clubs, etc.

Most people are surprised when they see just how long the list becomes. The next stage is to select those on the list with whom they would be most comfortable working. For a developmental alliance, they could use the mentor characteristics listed in Chapter 9 as an initial sorting system. They can then shortlist the most likely people and approach them to discuss the possibility of a developmental alliance.

Mentees should beware of eliminating people before considering them properly. A developmental alliance is an unusual arrangement, and it is surprising how many people have qualities that we overlook on a day-to-day basis, especially if our contacts with them have a different purpose. Many people are natural counsellors, so there will also be many who are instinctive mentors. There will be even more who have the necessary interest in other human beings and can develop the skills required.

This MLM technique can also be particularly useful if you want a mentor yourself, or if you work in a small company where existing working relationships make it difficult to find a mentor with the necessary degree of detachment. If you are independent, or 'between engagements', you might seek out colleagues who are also freelance or temporarily unemployed; you might also look for a mentor within any organizations with which you have contact. For independents, these might be companies with which you have contracts as a supplier. Professional networks are also a good place to look.

Those between jobs can still seek mentors, and indeed this might be the time when they have the greatest need. Our own development is often brought much more clearly into focus at times when we realize that organizations no longer promise jobs for life. Contact with a career or outplacement counsellor may resemble mentoring but will probably be closer to spot mentoring, because the focus is so specific.

Training

This book has not been written as a training manual. However, experienced trainers should have little difficulty in extracting suitable ideas and linking them with the content of other interpersonal skills training. Training should cover underpinning knowledge, models for sharing, core skills and situational skills.

Underpinning knowledge includes theories which help mentors (and mentees) to understand the process. Examples are the learning and changing frameworks in Chapter 11 and the overview of the stages of an alliance. *Models for sharing* may incorporate the same models as for underpinning knowledge, but will also encompass the theories for understanding mentee styles outlined in Chapter 9 and the various frameworks described in Chapter 10. *Situational skills* are spelt out in Chapter 8, while the core skills such as listening, questioning, reflecting and feedback are covered in many training materials related to counselling or appraisal skills.

It is important to consider the training needs of both mentors and mentees. Indeed, training mentees alone could have a significant impact, especially where it has not been feasible to shift traditional mentors across to a transformational mentoring style. For example, I recently completed a project to train new graduates within a City bank in *reverse* coaching skills. This came about because the dealers who were meant to be showing them the job were not always the most enthusiastic coaches. Equipping the graduates with appropriate skills enabled them to coach the coaches! It also had an impact on the general atmosphere in the dealing rooms.

I have already mentioned that much of this book will be relevant for anyone setting out to create their own developmental alliance. I have also concentrated on models for human growth and development, as I believe these are the key to successfully balancing the different aspects of our lives. So far, though, I have not provided much 'hard' information about what competences might be needed.

As part of the knowledge component, mentors and mentees are likely to need familiarity with the latest trends in competence-based ways of measuring development. There are now any number of lists of such competences, such as S/NVQ units and elements, plus professional association requirements. There has also been much research into the nature of management, the application of interpersonal skills and the implementation of team working approaches.

Rather than summarize here a lot of information which you can obtain elsewhere and may already know, I list below a set of core characteristics which I believe will be needed by successful executives, professionals, managers, teamleaders and most 'ordinary' knowledge workers in the future. These qualities are the result of research conducted more than a decade ago, in a British Airways department of 15 000 employees, some time before redundancies reduced them below 8000. The project included an extensive review of similar research and led to the conclusion that there were certain key characteristics which have been emerging under different labels over many years[6,7]. It seems highly probable that the list below will provide a basis for anyone who wants to function healthily in our current fast-moving work climate.

Factor A   Response to change
Responds positively to change, whether of people, procedures, tasks, constraints or objectives. Initiates change, seeks change as opportunity. Uses skills to position and reposition self to suit changing circumstances. Is adaptable, flexible and enjoys the challenge of change.

Factor B   Sense of Responsibility
Expects and accepts responsibility for self, others, the organization, the environment. Is decisive and proactive without infringing the rights and responsibilities of others. Considers and acts for the greater good of the community.

Factor C   Impact
Behaves confidently and assertively. Comes over as in command of self and situation. Exercises power and influence to have an impact on other people.

Factor D   Conceptualizing
Diagnoses, collects and analyses information. Looks for links, develops new ideas and constructs. Manages complexity and ambiguity.

Factor E   Multiple perspectives
Shows interest in the perspectives of others. Can combine and contrast different views, different disciplines. Understands own part in the whole, sees the total picture.

Factor F   Prediction
Looks ahead, seeks to forecast and predict. Prepares, plans, recognizes and acts in advance of obstacles. Reads the environment for trends. Proactive mindset.

Factor G   Respect and responsiveness
Recognizes the worth of others, respects their contributions. Spends time on relationships. Empathizes. Acts in ways that empower people.

Factor H   Communicating
Recognizes the need to communicate and does so consistently. Puts effort into making contact, formally and informally. Keeps people informed. Shares the vision.

Factor I   Self-awareness
Monitors own performance and impact on others. Is open and honest, admits shortcomings and uses feedback to learn. Self-aware and self-analytical.

These characteristics are not to be confused with skills and knowledge. They are *orientations*—evidence for them can be observed in behaviour, but the orientation itself is deeper. Provided we have the inclination towards these qualities, we can acquire the skills; without the orientation we may actually possess the skills, but not apply them unless someone in authority directs us to do so.

The orientations provide a useful basis for developmental alliances. They are the qualities we will need if we are to operate effectively in a world full of change. Whether we are working inside or outside an organizational setting, we will still have to manage our own growth— and we will increasingly want to do that in ways which are ethical and responsible. Individuals and organizations are all part of the greater whole, and each has an obligation to consider the broader implications of their actions.

Supporting

In addition to training, mentors will need ongoing support. For this we can borrow ideas from social work supervision. The case study discussion with one or more colleagues can be adapted. For one-to-one sessions, the mentor meets with a fellow mentor, or an experienced facilitator, to talk through current personal mentoring activity. For group support, several mentors get together to 'share and care'—each taking a turn at describing current mentoring activity and getting feedback, support and challenge from the others present. This has some similarity to an action learning set[8] or even to a therapy group.

Another option is to use the 'cascade'. In this, one person (B) 'supervises' (i.e. listens, questions, challenges, helps analyse) another mentor (A) about mentoring of a mentee. Then another person (C) supervises B about the way B helped A. Yet another person (D) may then supervise C about the way C's supervision helped B. Cascades like this are very effective at bringing out issues that are initially overlooked.

The same approaches can be applied to mentees. They, too, might spend time with a facilitator, although care must be taken that they do not start relating to the facilitator as if that person were the mentor instead. Mentee support groups will also be useful. For these, there must be an emphasis on discovering ways in which the mentee can function more effectively, so as to continually develop the relationship with the mentor. The support groups must avoid degenerating into a 'complain-about-the-mentor' session.

Support of a different kind can come to mentors and mentees through the way in which developmental alliances are viewed within an organiza-tion or professional group. If this style of mentoring is seen as new and challenging, those engaged in it will be rewarded through reputation and status. If, on the other hand, it is regarded as yet another idea from the personnel department, it will be avoided.

The reputation of such a mentoring approach can be enhanced through the same methods as are used to create new identities for organizations. These include the creation of new histories or traditions— an apparent contradiction which signifies that we have to provide special events that can be talked about. The British Airways 'Putting People First' sessions were like this—employees were taken in large numbers to plush surroundings, talked to by extremely capable presenters, fed exceptionally well, addressed by the Chief Executive, and sent away talking about the PPF events so that they became a milestone on the road to a new corporate identity.

The equivalent for a mentoring approach is to have briefings of a high standard, in surroundings that are the best available, with facilitators who are enthusiastic about the concept and with the presence of the Chief Executive at some point to display commitment. Another facet will be to use specific documentation, perhaps with a logo or some other sign of identification, so that the mentoring scheme takes on an identity of its own.

Consolidating transformation

Another paradox! Transformation means continuing to develop, so how can we consolidate it? What we can do is to establish some new *rites*— the patterns of activity that come to be associated with particular cultures. Organizations that change successfully generally do so by creating new rites and then introducing them quickly and with maximum impact. In this way they create 'new traditions'—they change the fables and myths, the ways that people talk about the organization, the ways that people think and feel about the organization. We all know the impact of stories about the good old days; if we provide more exciting new events to be talked about we can make a major shift in perceptions.

We can identify three stages based on anthropology where rites are significant: separation from the old, transition to the new, and incorporation of the new[9]. Based on this, we can therefore design and initiate a series of rites which relate to developmental alliances. Each needs to include some specific behaviours which people learn to use and which 'separate' them from others who have not undergone the rites. For maximum impact, each rite should also have some element of celebration that marks successful completion.

- *Rites of entry*: How do people become selected as mentors and mentees, what processes are there for excluding unsuitable candidates from a corporate group?

- *Rites of pairing*: What steps are used to match mentors with mentees, how do they get to know each other, how do they set about bonding and contracting with each other?
- *Rites of development*: How are they trained and how do they develop themselves to shift from traditional to transformational mentoring, how do they maintain the learning process throughout the mentoring relationship?
- *Rites of passage*: What do they do as they work through the stages of mentoring, how do they mark the ending of each stage and the movement into the next?
- *Rites of consolidation*: How do they appraise their relationship, how do they give each other feedback about the process, what do they do to ensure continuous development of their skills as mentor or mentee?
- *Rites of conclusion*: How do they plan the ending of the mentoring relationship, how do they celebrate successes, what do they do during the final session?

The rites for transformational mentoring will be different from the rites for a traditional approach. The more developed and specific they become, the more they will be associated with a particular format and the more they will reinforce the identity of this approach in the minds of those involved and the onlookers. The successful introduction of such 'new traditions' will help to ensure that developmental alliances are seen as contributing to the transformation of the organization.

Notes

1. Kets de Vries, Manfred F. R. and Miller, Danny, *The Neurotic Organization*, Jossey-Bass, 1984.
2. Egan, Gerard, *Adding Value: A Systematic Guide to Business-Based Management and Leadership*, Jossey-Bass, 1993.
3. Schaef, Anne Wilson and Fassel, Diane, *The Addictive Organization*, Harper, 1988.
4. Guest, David, Professor of Occupational Psychology, Birkbeck College, London, in letter to *Personnel Management Plus*, June 1994.
5. Metcalfe, David, Fernie, Sue and Woodland, Steve, *1991 Workplace Industrial Relations Survey*, London School of Economics, 1994.
6. Hay, Julie, *Identification of Core Characteristics and Development of a Concomitant Organizational Paradigm*, M. Phil. thesis, Henley/Brunel, 1988.
7. Hay, Julie, 'Managerial Competences or Managerial Characteristics', in *Management Education and Development*, Vol. 21, Part 5, pages 305–15, 1990.

8. For more information about action learning sets, see any books by the originator, Reg Revans.
9. Beyer, Janice M. and Trice, Harrison M., 'The Communication of Power Relations in Organizations through Cultural Rites', in Jones, Michael Owen *et al*, *Inside Organizations*, Sage, 1988.

Mentoring network

This network is for anyone interested in the future of mentoring, and particularly in new approaches to reflect the realities of flatter organizations, the implications of culture and gender and the relevance of mentoring for 'ordinary' people as well as selected fast trackers. The purpose of the network is to share ideas and information about non-traditional mentoring, ways in which this can be used to develop individuals and the links with change and corporate cultures.

The first meeting took place on 17 September 1992, and consisted largely of people who had been contacted by Julie Hay as part of research into books being written for publication by McGraw-Hill. At that first meeting it was agreed that quarterly meetings would take place on the first Wednesday in January, April, July and October, running from 1030 to 1530 to make it easier for those travelling long distances. Venues depend on offers to act as host.

There are a number of organizations involved, including banks, utilities, government agencies and departments, manufacturing and retail.

For more information contact A D International, Sherwood House, 7 Oxhey Road, Watford WD1 4QF, UK. Tel: 01923 224737 Fax: 01923 210648.

2 Organizational transformation

When a reviewer of the manuscript for this book suggested that I give a definition of OT, I was forced to confess to my editor that I had deliberately avoided this because it would be too hard to write! This appendix is the result of their persuasion to do my best.

So what is OT? Transformation refers to radical changes—so that what is changed takes on a significantly different form. Harrison Owen[1] gives the example of a caterpillar turning into a butterfly. He suggests that transformation is a process which occurs as an organization moves from one phase of its existence to another.

Another way of considering transformation is to look at the level, or depth, of change. The minimal level of change is to what we do, or to where and/or when we do it. The next level is more strategic, when we change how we do something and/or why we do it. Transformation comes when we change who we are rather than what we do. This is change at the level of our identity. It may well have a spiritual dimension involving a shift in the way we feel connected to other people, to a higher consciousness, to nature and so on.

Organizational transformation is therefore about the *identity* of an organization. It will involve elements such as the vision and the mission statement, the values of the organization, the ways in which all stakeholders are treated and the relationships between the organization and its environment. Frank Rose, writing in *Fortune* magazine on 30 October 1990, suggested that a transforming organization would have moved beyond communications training and team building. Instead, the focus would be on deeper issues, such as the myths and rituals which contribute to the spirit of the organization.

In Chapter 2 I have given some other ideas about the distinction between change and transformation. I hope that this also provides a 'flavour' of the differences. Another way to consider OT is to look at the impact on management styles—OT implies a shift:

- from controlling to coaching
- from managing to mentoring

and is based on the notion that we have gone from:

■ organization to organism

as our metaphor.

Finally, if you want to know more about OT, see a collection of readings on the subject edited by John D. Adams[2].

Notes

1. Owen, Harrison, *Spirit: Transformation and Development in Organizations*, Abbotts Publishing, 1987.
2. Adams, John D. (ed), *Transforming Work*, Miles River Press, 1984.

3 | 12-step mentoring

We can link the shadow side, addictive nature of organizations and the individuals within them to the well-known 12-step programme applied by Alcoholics Anonymous (AA). The 12-step programme is already used for addictions other than alcohol, it has been developed and refined over more than half a century and it works for an estimated 50 per cent of those using it (who in 1992 numbered 1.5 million in 131 countries![1]).

We can convert it to provide a set of steps[2] which can be applied to organizational settings. I have reworded the 12 steps for this purpose, with acknowledgements to AA (the original version is widely known and can be obtained from local branches or the address given at the end of this chapter)[3].

Step 1   We admitted that we had been unable to solve a problem that was seriously undermining our quality of life

This represents the initial acceptance by mentees that they have a problem which needs to be tackled. This may involve recognizing that their long working hours are excessive, that their failure to take annual holidays is unhealthy, or that the level of competitiveness in the organization is preventing genuine human contact with colleagues.

It is important at this stage to take a careful look at the organizational culture. Workaholics are frequently encouraged and rewarded, especially in 'macho' companies where people boast about how hard they work, how late they stay, what pressure they deal with. Even the training course may reinforce such a message, with trainers expecting participants to work late into the night—overlooking the fact that little learning actually takes place then.

Questions[4] which might be useful at this stage include:

- Are there aspects of my behaviour that regularly lead to problems?
- Have other people confronted (or attempted to confront) me about my dysfunctional patterns of behaviour?
- Do people make jokes or sarcastic comments about my working style?

Step 2   We came to believe that a power greater than ourselves could restore us to healthy functioning

This relates to recognition of a larger reality and that there is more to life than our own narrow commitment to our addiction. There is something spiritual about the way in which mentors are willing to give their time to help mentees grow and develop. This caring without material reward is a great example of human generosity of spirit.

The greater power can equally be interpreted as referring to an inner strength and wisdom, as well as to an external concept of God. The AA version emphasizes that the greater power is not tied to any religion, but is whatever we understand it to be.

Questions:

- What do I really want in my life?
- How can I reconnect with my inner strength, the community offered me by others, the collective unconscious, or whatever else I believe in?
- How can my relationship with my mentor be a source of support as I overcome my addiction?

Step 3 We made a decision to tune into and act upon that greater power (or inner wisdom)

This step is about recognizing that we have more resources available to us than we first believed. Making a decision to use the mentoring process reflects an acceptance of the help being offered to us by another human being—that our connection within the human race has a spiritual element.

For many women, it may instead be more important to emphasize the way in which a mentor can stimulate us to get in touch with our own inner resources. This will counteract any tendency to accept the cultural expectations that women are dependent and cannot solve problems themselves[5].

Questions:

- What stops me from trusting my own inner wisdom?
- What stops me from accepting the genuine caring and support that is offered me by my mentor?
- What stops me from recognizing that the developmental alliance is part of being connected to something greater than the sum of the parts?

Step 4 We made a searching and fearless moral inventory of ourselves

This step is the assessment stage of mentoring, extended to include a thorough review of the ways in which workaholism or other addictions affect all aspects of the mentee's life.

It is worth noting, however, that we need to guard against seeing healthy functioning a problem. Those who fail to adopt the addictive norms of an organization are often seen as the ones at fault. Rejecting the macho culture, for example, may lead to criticism about lack of assertiveness; living a balanced lifestyle may be regarded incorrectly as lack of commitment in a workaholic company.

Questions:

■ What are my strengths and weaknesses?
■ What are the benefits I gain from my weaknesses?
■ What are the potential drawbacks associated with my strengths?

Step 5   We brought our shortcomings into awareness and shared this with another human being

Admitting our problems requires a high level of trust in the mentor and commitment to the relationship. Telling another person about our difficulties is often a major breakthrough, particularly when we realize that they continue to be supportive rather than blaming.

At this point we will also need to forgive ourselves. Our mentor can help us to put things into perspective, so that we come to understand that everyone has some areas of their life that they would prefer to deny. Our 'wrongs' are, in fact, our adaptations—ways of behaving that we chose when we were little because we believed at the time that it was the only way to survive.

Questions:

■ How do I feel when I tell someone else about my problems?
■ How has keeping my shortcomings a secret prevented me from developing more healthy options?
■ How have these behaviour patterns served me in the past, when I believed I had no other options?

Step 6   We accepted that we could change, with help and support

Here we accept that change is possible and that we will be better able to change if we accept the support offered to us within the mentoring relationship.

Questions:

■ What am I going to change?
■ How can I use the caring and concern of the mentor to support me in making changes?

Step 7   We decided to use our spiritual resources as a source of change

Having accepted that we can change, we still need to make a definite commitment to do so by using our own inner strengths, by accepting the supportive nature of the mentoring relationship and by drawing on whatever greater power we believe in.

Questions:

- How can I draw psychological support from the nature of the developmental alliance?
- Where else can I find support?
- How will my beliefs support me in making changes?

Step 8   We made a list of all persons we had harmed, and became willing to make amends to them

This step fits into the alternatives stage of a developmental alliance. This and the next step are an important part of the 12-step process and should not be overlooked.

Questions:

- Who are the people I feel most uncomfortable towards?
- What have I done that I regret?

Step 9   We made direct amends to such people wherever possible, except when to do so would cause yet more problems

This step can be dealt with during the action planning phase of mentoring. Mentees may well need extra support from the mentor as they take action on step 9, especially as the 'injured parties' may be unwilling to accept any attempts to make amends.

Questions:

- How difficult will it be for me to approach them again to make amends?
- In what ways can I best make amends for past transgressions?

Step 10   We continued to take personal inventory and accept responsibility for our shortcomings

Having completed the earlier steps, it is important to maintain the momentum. People are rarely able to cease their addiction at the first attempt—if they were, then more of them would do so. Our workaholism or other addictive behaviours have usually been reinforced as a pattern over many years, so we need some time to substitute other ways of behaving.

The advantage of having a mentoring relationship which extends over many months is that the mentor can continue to be a strong source of support as the mentee struggles with the changes to a non-addictive lifestyle.

Questions:

- What will I do to review my progress on a regular basis?
- How will I use the mentoring relationship to help me?
- In what ways can I 'confess' further shortcomings so that I stay focused on resolving them?

Step 11   We continued to trust, honour and act on our spiritual wisdom

Eventually, the mentoring relationship will end, and mentees will need to handle their difficulties on their own. To do otherwise might lead to a dependency relationship, with mentees believing that they can only deal with their addiction if they can rely on their mentors. This step therefore highlights the need for mentees to develop their own inner resources, in whatever way they choose.

Questions:

- How do I view the purpose of my life now?
- What changes shall I make to maintain my new behaviour patterns?
- What strengths have I identified within myself?
- How will I continue to spend time with myself, meditating or otherwise getting in touch with my inner processes?

Step 12   Having had a spiritual awakening as a result of these steps, we will carry the message to other addicts and practise the principles ourselves

A mentee in a developmental alliance experiences at first hand how powerful it can be to have the full support and attention of another human being who is not seeking anything in return. This is the spiritual element of mentoring, where people exhibit a genuine level of caring for another.

Having experienced the benefits, it is to be hoped that mentees will, in turn, offer to be mentors to others. It can be particularly helpful, for example, if recovered workaholics are willing to help others face the same addictions. This is a major strength of AA, where everyone has faced similar difficulties.

Questions:

- How do I feel about other people knowing of my struggles—and successes?
- How will I share my own experiences of change with others?

■ How will I explain my understanding of God, or a higher power, or the spirituality of the mentoring connection?

Rescuer or facilitator

Using something as powerful as the 12-step model requires us to be wary of entering into the psychological games that get played around and with addicts. Steve Karpman[6] gave us the concept of the *drama triangle* as a way of understanding these dynamics. In this, those involved take on roles as Persecutors, Rescuers or Victims. The game payoff comes as they shift positions—for example, the addict behaves like a helpless victim, someone feels obliged to rescue him or her, and the end result is that Rescuer or Victim moves to Persecutor.

In the workplace, for example, the workaholic takes on far too much work and then behaves as if they had no choice and cannot possibly get everything done in time (Victim). The Rescuer starts off with helpful suggestions, or even offers to do some of the work. The Victim rejects all of these suggestions. If the Victim accepts the offer of help, they are likely later to complain that the work has been done incorrectly. The Victim thus acts like a Persecutor, while the Rescuer shifts to Victim as ideas or work belonging to them are ridiculed. The alternative ending occurs when the Rescuer becomes frustrated, loses patience and persecutes the Victim.

Mentors often have Rescuer tendencies! It will be particularly important that they guard against these when mentoring workaholics (and if they suspect that their mentee is an alcoholic). The alternative involves ensuring that they opt for a positive, healthy set of options as shown in Figure A3.1.

Responsible instead of Rescuer

This means being responsible for other people, not ignoring real persecution, not adopting a bystander role in the face of oppression, but avoiding potential 'gamey' behaviour by checking that the Victim is working just as hard as you are to solve the problem.

One simple way to achieve this is to ask people what options they have considered, what they have tried already, what factors they think are significant. It will soon become apparent if they are not putting any effort into solving the problem themselves.

Powerful instead of Persecutor

This is about using reasonable power to take action and to express views. It is the converse of persecuting, which is using power to punish or coerce

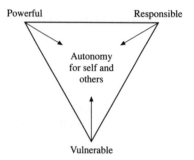

Figure A3.1 *The autonomy triangle.*

people. Persecutors aim to put others into a one-down position; when we are healthily powerful we are assertive and our goal is a win–win outcome.

There are many books on assertiveness which explore this option in detail. Put simply, it usually requires that we understand and respect the maps of reality held by other people, while at the same time insisting that they cease behaviour which impinges on the rights of us or third parties.

Vulnerable instead of Victim

The third corner of the triangle concerns our ability to be honest about our shortcomings and concerns. Psychological Victims are people who have lost touch with their real needs and are therefore unwittingly using manoeuvres to get other people to pay attention to them.

Being open to emotions and recognizing that everyone has some weaknesses will allow us to accept the fallibility of ourselves and other people. This will permit us to empathize when mentees are struggling. It will also enable us to model healthy ways of admitting our deeper concerns.

Notes

1. Figures quoted by Robbins, Lee, 'Designing more Functional Organizations: The 12-Step Model', in *Journal of Organizational Change Management*, Vol. 5, No. 4, pages 41–58. This is also an excellent article about the potential benefits of the 12-Step programme for organizations.
2. The idea of relating the 12 steps to workaholism in this way came from a conference presentation and conversation with Weiss, Laurie, co-author with Weiss, Jonathon, of *Recovery from Co-Dependency*, Health Communications Inc., 1989.

3. AA World Services are at 468 Park Avenue South, New York, NY 10016, USA.
4. The questions given for each step were stimulated by ideas for linking Tarot symbols to the 12 steps, contained in Grant, Richard D., *Symbols of Recovery: The Twelve Steps at Work in the Unconscious*, Type and Temperament Inc., 1990.
5. The conversion of AA 12 Steps to counteract cultural norms about women's behaviour is suggested by Kasl, Charlotte, in *Many Roads, One Journey: Moving Beyond the Twelve Steps*, Harper & Row, 1992.
6. Karpman, Stephen, 'Fairy Tales and Script Drama Analysis', in *Transactional Analysis Bulletin*, 7(26), pages 39–43, 1968.

Bibliography

Aburdene, Patricia and Naisbitt, John, *Megatrends for Women*, Random House, 1993.

Adams, John D. (ed), *Transforming Work*, Miles River Press, 1984.

Bannister, D. and Fransella, F., *Inquiring Man: The Theory of Personal Constructs*, Penguin, 1971.

Barham, Kevin and Rassain, Clive, Ashbridge Management Research Group, *Shaping the Corporate Future*, Unwin Hyman Ltd, 1989.

Barry, David, 'Managing the Bossless Team: Lessons in Distributed Leadership', in *Organizational Dynamics*, Summer 1991, pages 31–47.

Berne, Eric, *A Layman's Guide to Psychiatry and Psychoanalysis*, Penguin, 1971.

Beyer, Janice M. and Trice, Harrison M., 'The Communication of Power Relations in Organizations through Cultural Rites', in Jones, Michael Owen *et al.*, *Inside Organizations*, Sage, 1988.

Bloch, Susan, 'Business Mentoring and Coaching', in *Training and Development*, April 1993.

Bohm, D., *Wholeness and the Implicate Order*, Routledge and Kegan Paul, 1980.

Boyer, Isabel, *Flexible Working for Managers*, Chartered Institute of Management Accountants, 1993.

Bretto, Charlotte C., *A Framework for Excellence*, 1988, reproduced with permission as *Practitioner Training Manual 1992* by Pace Personal Development Ltd, London.

Buzan Tony, *Make the Most of Your Mind*, Pan Books, 1981.

Charlesworth, Paul, 'Don't Lose your Valuable Staff', in *Professional Manager*, May 1994.

Chew, G. F., 'Bootstrap: A Scientific Idea?' in *Science*, 161, 1968, pages 762–65.

Clarkson, Petruska, *Gestalt Counselling in Action*, Sage, 1989.

Clarkson, Petruska, *Transactional Analysis Psychotherapy*, Routledge, 1992.

Clutterbuck, David, *Everyone Needs a Mentor*, Institute of Personnel Management, 2nd edn, 1991.

Egan, Gerard, *Adding Value: A Systematic Guide to Business-Based Management and Leadership*, Jossey-Bass, 1993.

Fletcher, Clive, *Appraisal: Routes to Improved Performance*, IPM, 1993.

Forrest, A. and Tolfree, P., *Leaders: The Learning Curve of Achievement*, Industrial Society, 1992.

Gallie, Duncan and White, Michael, *Employee Commitment and the Skills Revolution*, PSI Publishing/Policy Studies Institute (preliminary report of Employment in Britain Survey), 1993.

Golzen, Godfrey and Garner, Andrew, *Smart Moves: Successful Strategies and Tactics for Career Management*, Basil Blackwell, 1990.

Grant, Richard D., *Symbols of Recovery: The Twelve Steps at Work in the Unconscious*, Type and Temperament Inc., 1990.

Handy, Charles, *The Age of Unreason*, Business Books Ltd, 1989.

Handy, Charles, *The Empty Raincoat*, Hutchinson, 1994.

Harris, Thomas, *I'm OK, You're OK*, Pan, 1973.

Harrison, Roger, *Organisation Culture and Quality of Service: A Strategy for Releasing Love in the Workplace*, Association of Management Education and Development, 1987.

Hay, Julie, *Identification of Core Characteristics and Development of a Concomitant Organizational Paradigm*, M Phil thesis, Henley/Brunel, 1988.

Hay, Julie, 'Managerial Competences or Managerial Characteristics', in *Management Education and Development*, Vol. 21, Part 5, pages 305–15, 1990.

Hay, Julie, *Transactional Analysis for Trainers*, McGraw-Hill, 1992.

Hay, Julie, *Working it Out at Work—Understanding Attitudes and Building Relationships*, Sherwood, 1993.

Herriott, Peter, *The Career Management Challenge: Balancing Individual and Organizational Needs*, Sage, 1992.

Honey, Peter and Mumford, Alan, *The Manual of Learning Styles*, Peter Honey, 1986.

Howell, W. S., *The Empathic Communicator*, Wadsworth, 1982.

Institute of Management and Manpower PLC, *The Survey of Long-term Employment Strategies*, 1993 (available from the Institute of Management).

Jongeward, Dorothy and Seyer, Philip, *Choosing Success*, John Wiley & Sons Inc., 1978.

Kahler, Taibi, *Managing with the Process Communication Model*, Human Development Publications, 1979.

Karpman, Stephen, 'Fairy Tales and Script Drama Analysis', in *Transactional Analysis Bulletin*, 7(26), 1968, pages 39–43.

Kasl, Charlotte, *Many Roads, One Journey: Moving Beyond the Twelve Steps*, Harper & Row, 1992.

Kelley, Robert E., *The Gold-Collar Worker: Harnessing the Brainpower of the New Work Force*, Addison-Wesley, 1985.

Kelly, George, *The Psychology of Personal Constructs*, Norton, 1955.

Kets de Vries, Manfred F. R. and Miller, Danny, *The Neurotic Organization*, Jossey-Bass, 1984.

Kirton, Michael, *Adaptors and Innovators: Cognitive Style and Personality*, Hatfield Polytechnic, 1984.

Kolb, D. A., *Experiential Learning*, Prentice-Hall, 1984.

Laborde, Genie Z., *Influencing with Integrity*, Syntony Publishing, 1987.

Lawrence, Gordon, *People Types and Tiger Stripes*, Centre for Applications of Psychological Type Inc., 2nd edn, 1982.

Lester, Tom, 'The Gores' Happy Family', in *Management Today*, February 1993.

Levin, Pamela, *Becoming the Way We Are*, Health Communications Inc., 3rd edn, 1988.

Levin, Pamela, *Cycles of Power: A User's Guide to the Seven Seasons of Life*, Health Communications Inc., 1988.

Lynch, Dudley and Kordis, Paul L., *Strategy of the Dolphin*, Arrow Books, 1988.

McGoldrick, M. and Gerson, R., *Genograms in Family Assessment*, Norton, 1985.

McKewn, Jennifer, 'Modern Gestalt—an Integrative and Ethical Approach to Counselling and Psychotherapy' in *The Journal of the British Association for Counselling*, Vol. 5, No. 2, May 1994.

Metcalfe, David, Fernie, Sue and Woodland, Steve, *1991 Workplace Industrial Relations Survey*, London School of Economics, 1994.

Micholt, Nelly, 'Psychological Distance and Group Interventions', in *Transactional Analysis Journal*, Vol. 22, No. 4, October 1992, pages 228–33.

Morgan, Gareth, *Images of Organization*, Sage, 1986.

Morgan, Gareth, *Imaginization*, Sage, 1993.

Myers Briggs, Isabel, *Gifts Differing*, Consulting Psychologists Press Inc., 1980.

Owen, Harrison, *Spirit: Transformation and Development in Organizations*, Abbotts Publishing, 1987.

Peck, M. Scott, *The Different Drum*, Rider & Co., 1987.

Pedler, Mike, Burgoyne, John and Boydell, Tom, *The Learning Company*, McGraw-Hill, 1991.

Peter, Laurence J. and Hull, Raymond, *The Peter Principle: Why Things Always Go Wrong*, Souvenir Press, reissued 1992.

Peters, Tom, *Liberation Management*, Macmillan, 1992.

Popcorn, Faith, *The Popcorn Report*, Doubleday, 1991.

Robbins, Lee, 'Designing more Functional Organizations: The 12-Step Model', in *Journal of Organizational Change Management*, Vol. 5, No. 4, 1992, pages 41–58.

Rogers, Carl, *Client-Centred Therapy*, Constable & Co Ltd, 1951.

Sadler, Philip, 'Gold Collar Workers: what makes them play their best?', *Personnel Management*, April 1994.

Schaef, Anne Wilson and Fassel, Diane, *The Addictive Organization*, HarperSanFrancisco, 1988.

Semler, Ricardo, *Maverick*, Century, 1993.

Spooner, Adrian, 'Mentoring and Flexible Training', in *Management Development Review*, Vol. 6, No. 2, 1993, pages 21–25.

Steiner, Claude, *Scripts People Live*, Bantam Books, 1975.

Stewart, I. and Joines, V., *TA Today*, Lifespace Publishing, 1988.

Stewart, A. and Stewart, R., *Tomorrows' Men Today*, IPM, 1977 (since reissued as *Tomorrow's Managers Today*).

Storey, John, Okasaki-Ward, Lola, Sisson, Keith *et al.*, *Managers and Management Development in Britain and Japan*, Basil Blackwell, 1992.

Tannen, Deborah, *You Just Don't Understand Me*, Virago Press, 1991.

Weiss, Laurie and Weiss, Jonathon, *Recovery from Co-Dependency*, Health Communications Inc., 1989.

Index